# Holoflux: Codex

# Holoflux: Codex

**Form/Movement/Vision**
*~inspired by~*
**David Bohm**

## Contributors

Richard Burg
Sky Hoorne
Maria Hvidbak
Beth Macy
Hester Reeve
Aja Bulla Zamastil

**Edited by Lee Nichol**

Pari Publishing

Copyright © 2022 The Pari Center for compilation.
Copyright © 2022 All contributors for words and images.

All rights reserved. No part of this publication may be reproduced, transmitted or stored in a retrieval system, in any form or by any means, without permission in writing from Pari Publishing Sas, application for which must be made to the publisher.

ISBN 987-88-95604-36-7

Book and cover design: Lee Nichol and Eva Leong Casey
Cover art: *Heliac*, acrylic on canvas (detail) by Eva Leong Casey
Layout: Eva Leong Casey

**Pari Publishing**
Via Tozzi 7, 58045 Pari (GR), Italy
www.paripublishing.com

Printed in China, November 2022

# Contents

Introduction ............................................................. vii

**Sky** ........................................... 1, 45, 83, 115, 179, 233
Sky Hoorne

**From Mountain to Sea** ......................................... 9
Aja Bulla Zamastil

**Letters of Philosophy** ........................................ 51
Maria Hvidbak

**Bohmian Art School Revolution** ..................... 89
Hester Reeve

**Intermezzo** ........................................................ 123
Beth Macy

**Releasement** .................................................... 187
Richard Burg

**Afterword** ........................................................ 239

**Coda** ................................................................. 242

**Acknowledgements** ......................................... 245

**Appendices** ..................................................... 247

# Introduction

> The new form of insight can perhaps best be called *Undivided Wholeness in Flowing Movement*. This view implies that flow is, in some sense, prior to that of the "things" that can be seen to form and dissolve in this flow.
>
> — David Bohm, *Wholeness and the Implicate Order*

It is not an easy thing, or a simple thing, to come to the boundary of how we imagine ourselves. Our identities are put together in such fashion as to guard against such trespass. Beyond that boundary, we suspect, lie uncertainty and confusion—even chaos and dissolution. Better to stick with the known, than to probe into the unknown.

If we do attempt to venture beyond, we quickly encounter a multitude of conservative anchors, well-set and ready to hold us in place as we are. There is the entirety of our personal history—all of our experiences, all of our memories, all of our accumulated meanings. More broadly, there are the cultures in which we have been raised, and the potent, unseen ways in which we have been shaped by these cultures. Beyond that lies the deep time of our ancestral streams, dreamlike, rarely recognized, yet subtly informing how we find ourselves placed in the world.

All of these factors come into play, overtly or tacitly, if we arrive at the boundary of how we imagine ourselves. And for good reason—these identity structures provide us with grounding, with reference points, with orientation. They allow us to create lives of relative authenticity and inner meaning, both individually and culturally. To trespass these boundaries—to dislodge the anchors—really does expose us to the unknown, in profound and unexpected ways. This is not an idle concern. But at various historical junctures, the boundaries of identity and order can begin to fray of their own accord. As the poet Yeats forewarned, "Things fall apart; the center cannot hold."

We are now in such a time. Social fragmentation is at a breaking point, with no relief in sight. Climate change has morphed into climate emergency, seemingly overnight. Information technology, artificial intelligence, and bio-engineering follow rules of their own, largely unmoored from even short-term implications. Forced migration has exploded worldwide. Wealth inequality has gone off the rails.

The imminent convergence of these trends does not bode well. To the contrary—it is difficult to imagine a more toxic global environment on the near horizon. It is clear that action must be taken, immediately, from many quarters, to forestall the very real "tipping points" that we are often warned about. Without such action at every level—individual, collective, global—our prospects seem very dim indeed.

It is in this historical context that the existential inquiries of the late physicist David Bohm hold a significant place. As early as 1980, Bohm indicated that the circumstances in which we currently find ourselves were all but inevitable. And though he was a proponent of any and all actions that could forestall calamity, he pointed to a source—hiding in plain view—that he felt to be at the root of our current challenges. This source is the activity of human thought, and the manner in which it has evolved over millennia. The core characteristic of this thought is that it displays a world of independent, self-existing *things*—dogs, tangerines, cars, atoms, trees, galaxies, human beings, forks, meteorites, mountains, cows, carpets, clocks. Things!

We are so profoundly acclimated to seeing the world in this way that it is nearly impossible to imagine it any other way. The fragmented world displayed by thought is so self-evident that it warrants no consideration—a classic feedback loop that appears innocuous in its daily particulars. But when we take a sustained look at the larger social and ecological patterns that accrue from this ingrained fragmentation, the results, as indicated above, are breathtaking. And the correlate to seeing the world as consisting of things is equally fraught, and equally hidden away: we ourselves become a "thing"—a self-existing, independent object among all the others. We then have the "observer" (me, as a thing) and the "observed" (any and every thing other than me). With this, a firm self-referencing system is set in place, re-enacted by each of us, every day, every second of every day.

In Bohm's view, this recurring cycle of thing-ness and fragmentation underlies the modes of perception and action that result in our present crises. It is natural, when we experience the world as a collection of independent objects, to then conceive of the world mechanistically, and to become mechanistic in our behavior. This pervasive fragmentation filters out relationship, process, participation, wholeness—leading to further fragmentation, in a downward historical spiral. It is by grasping the entirety of this cycle—which is both individual and cultural—that we might come to realize the necessity of a radical change in the way our consciousness constructs a world. It is only a change of this magnitude, felt Bohm, that could lay the foundation for long-term coherence and stability, rather than erratic and topical "solutions"—however well-intended and necessary these latter may be.

There are many ways one can approach Bohm's proposals regarding the nature of consciousness. But whether we approach from the point of view of physics, or from the point of view of direct experience, we will find *movement* to be fundamental. The terms Bohm used to indicate this primacy of movement are *holomovement* and alternately, *holoflux*.

For those non-physicists interested in Bohm's work with consciousness, there have typically been two available avenues. One is his work with dialogue, with an emphasis on collective thought and meaning. The other is often more individualized, following his proposals regarding thought as a system and proprioception of thought. In either approach, there has been a tendency to sideline Bohm's emphasis on movement. On the one hand, it is easy to dismiss movement as something so obvious, so simple, that it can't really be all that significant. On the other hand, when one considers the implications of *holoflux*, it may seem too vast, too unreckonable.

And indeed, holoflux indicates something truly vast. In Bohm's metaphysics, it points to *all that is*—the fluxing, dynamic movement of the ever-emerging whole, of all that can possibly be. Holoflux "carries" and subsumes all he described as explicate orders, and all he described as implicate orders. Everything we think of as "world" and "cosmos" is perpetually unfolding from holoflux, from holomovement.

Indeed, Bohm suggested that there really are no "things" at all—only constellations and vortices of movement that temporarily appear as things (dogs, atoms, mountains, cows), only to eventually dissolve back into the flux from which they arose.

So yes, holoflux is vast—but it is also intimate. We too are perpetually unfolding from and re-enfolding into holoflux. Every particle of our physicality, every shading and nuance of our consciousness—all is unfolding from holoflux. In this view, our deepest nature, our primordial being, is movement, flux. Alas, for most of us, this is not how we experience the world. The world we inhabit—the world created by our thought—is the world of thing-ness.

It was just these considerations of movement, of holoflux, that inspired a small group of thirty or so people to embark on an experimental approach to Bohm's work. Sponsored by the Pari Center in Pari, Italy, we began with a program, "Entering Bohm's Holoflux." Rather than come to movement as a subset of dialogue, or a subset of proprioceptive awareness, we *began* with movement, placing it front and center. Our working hypothesis has been that if we can refine and deepen our innate sense of movement, other aspects of Bohm's proposals could be more intuitively understood—less abstract, more concrete, more embodied.

Among these other aspects is *meaning*. From the rudimentary mind-like qualities of the quantum realm, to the prospect of vast intelligences in the cosmos more generally, a Bohmian cosmos is shot through with meaning. By opening ourselves to such more-than-human meaning, felt Bohm, we might renew our capacities for relationship, for wholeness—and actively enter a participatory world. In our nascent holoflux experiments, testing these prospects began with movement.

The fulcrum around which these experiments turn is *rheosoma*, that is, the flowing body. In the first instance, "body" means our personal, individual body. What is the movement of the life-force within that body? How thoroughly can we attune to that? We thus begin very close to home, sensing the combinations and permutations of movement within us—literally. With this basis, we then extend the experiment "outward," into the world around us. If we can attune to that "outer" world *through* the movement we have discovered within us, what new dimensions of movement, relationship, and participation are revealed?

As our experiment unfolded, individuals began to give formal presentations to the group, using a variety of media to illustrate how they had been experiencing movement, *rheosoma*, and other glimmerings of holoflux. It soon became apparent that it might be useful to share these experiences beyond the confines of our working group. We determined early on that a printed book would be the most durable medium for this purpose, but we immediately faced a conundrum. How could the original multi-media presentations be made into a book? The answer was, they couldn't be. The solution was for each contributor to return to the wellsprings, and find a way of conveying their experience that would be oriented to the printed page.

But in keeping with our experiment, each person's experience was also in a process of flux, and had in most cases changed considerably, or even totally, from the time of the original presentations. Their contributions, then, reflect moments in time, already come and gone, though still very much alive. They are, to use a term from our experiments, *indefinities*—probings into increasingly subtle aspects of movement and flux.

It is our hope that a random image from the book, or some turn of phrase, could inspire further inquiry into the nature of movement, the nature of holoflux—which is our own nature. Such inquiry could reach beyond the theoretical, into the weave and warp of daily life. Finding our way back into "Bohmian" movement may indeed be challenging, as it necessarily involves questions of personal identity and orientation. But it also opens entirely new vistas of beauty and meaning, of coherence and wholeness. There is then the prospect that, rather than being pushed by historical forces to the boundary of how we imagine ourselves, we could do so intentionally, creatively. To come to this boundary knowingly, without resistance or conflict—this itself could be an inflection point in those forces which are otherwise poised to engender more fear, more divisiveness, more confusion.

And while it does seem that something very much along these lines is what David Bohm was concerned with, *Holoflux: Codex* is not a treatise on the work of Bohm. Nor is it an "art book" in any conventional sense. It is the documentation of six individuals, mid-stream in experimentation, inspired by Bohm—by his vision, his boundary-crossing, and his life-long reliance on movement and flux as the testing ground for all he brought forth.

Lee Nichol
October 2022
Albuquerque, New Mexico

# Sky 1

---

Sky Hoorne

*Is it not so…*

…that our upbringing, our outlook on life and the world, form and uphold the filters that guide our perceptual processes? The way we look at the whole will largely determine how we take in the parts, and which aspects of the whole are deemed important to recognize and record. If movement is primordial—as in the holoflux perspective—then surely the generative imagination that goes with it will yield different qualities than what a conventional mechanistic perspective presents us with…

*My attention is caught by the geese flying over our house in the evening. They sound so very up close with their typical noises, as if they are brushing by my ears in an intimate encounter. Their honking reverberates as if they are calling me to recognize my "gooseness," my creatureliness, luring me into the mystery of moving with the flow, flowing with the movement, cognitively and somatically fluxing in a non-local concerto. Attuning to them bodily, it becomes easier to realize how similar these animals are to one's own being, and to imagine moving as they do. In fact, we are not that different from birds, as we still carry the shared reptile ancestry in our brains and our flesh and bones…*

Generative, perception-forming imagination is commonly thought to be unconscious, uncontrollable and inaccessible, but is that actually so? Have there not been artists, mystics, scientists, and philosophers who influenced our shared imagery, who created and discovered new perspectives, new visions, new metaphors? Exploring the realm of holoflux, it appears that this creative source is available to each and every one of us, if only we pay sufficient attention and open up to it.

It is right in front of us all the time.

# From Mountain to Sea

---

Aja Bulla Zamastil

- something looking back at me - open to these larger movements to get out of ourselves, to find ourselves in a different way

when we look at trees we can also feel the echoes of what they have seen - what is behind the dense material experience inside the earth inside us - open to these larger movements to get out of ourselves, to find ourselves in a different way - open to this movement - then we may have a better chance of holding the difficulty of the world - of moving closer to becoming whole human beings

what is behind the dense material experience inside the earth inside us

can we hold the coolness and the fire – the tension within the flow

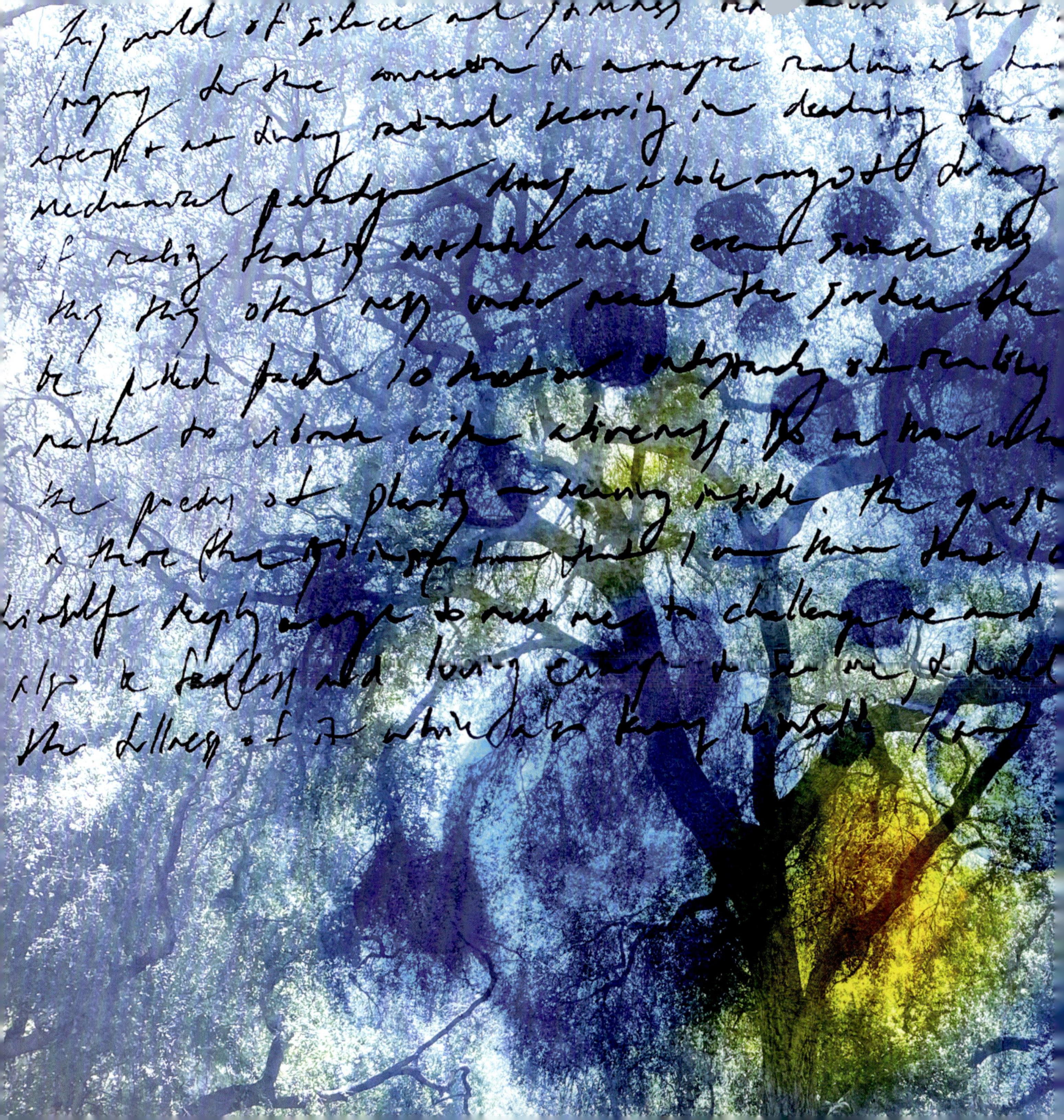

implicit light | explicate shadow

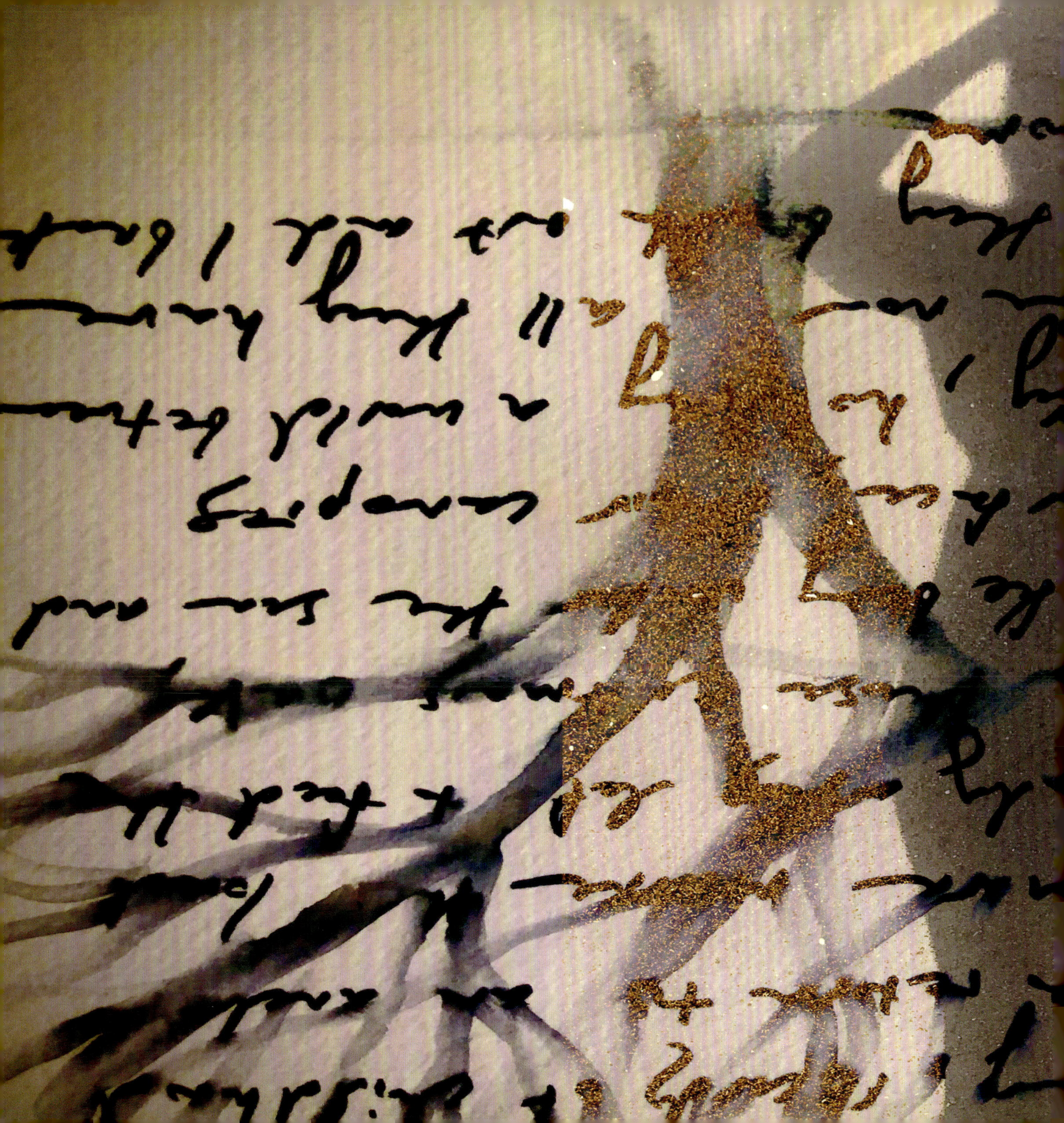

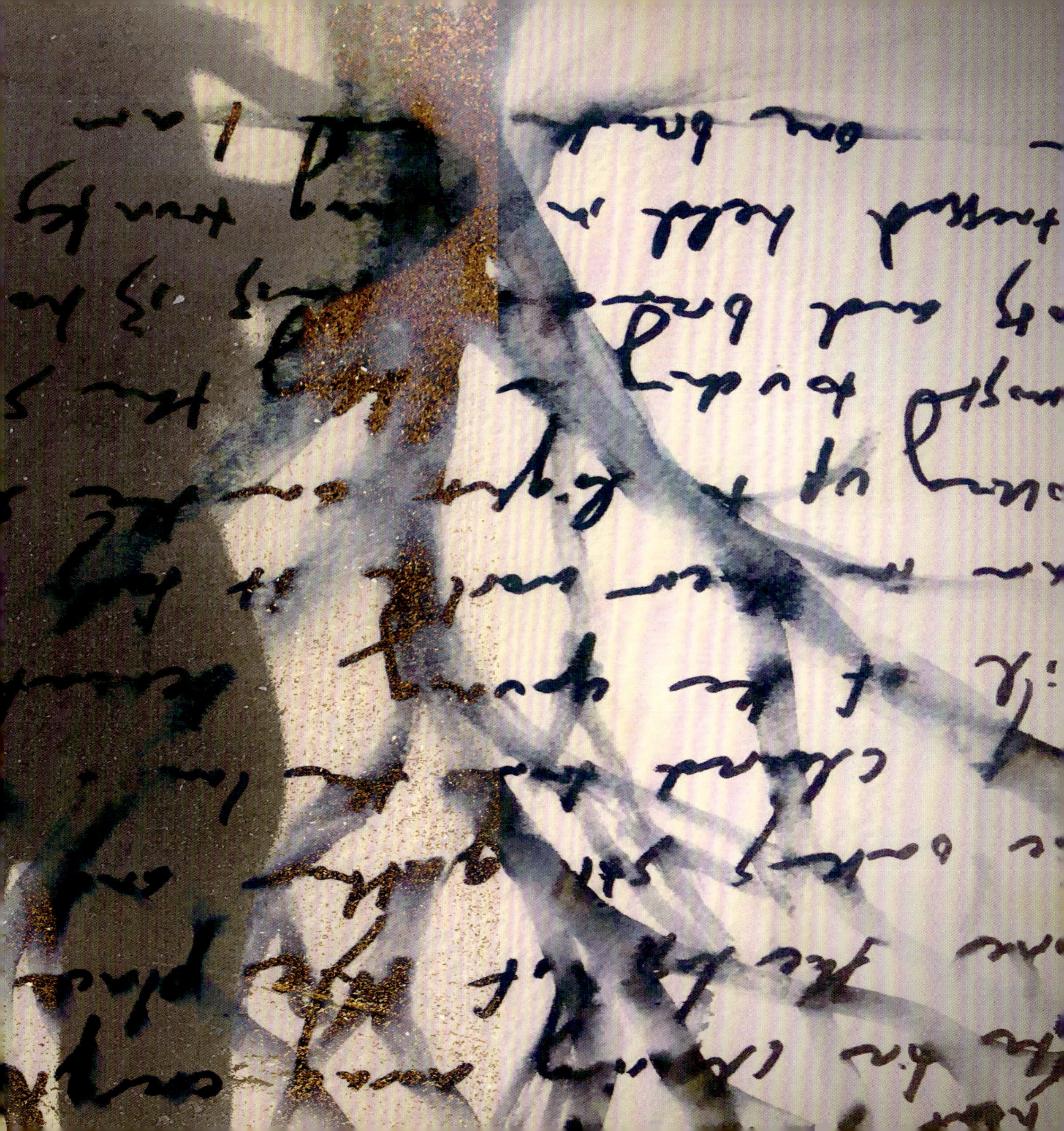

VENTURA

What is it that resists a quality of fullhearted joy? A deep upwelling from inside the earth, the water, the sun, unsettles my sense of me moving through life in a known world of things. Another movement pulls, without a reference point - an ineffable longing to be with the creatures of the earth, inside their pawing, crowing, calling, swimming, gazing at what is behind the dense material experience inside the earth inside us - open to these larger movements to find ourselves in a different way

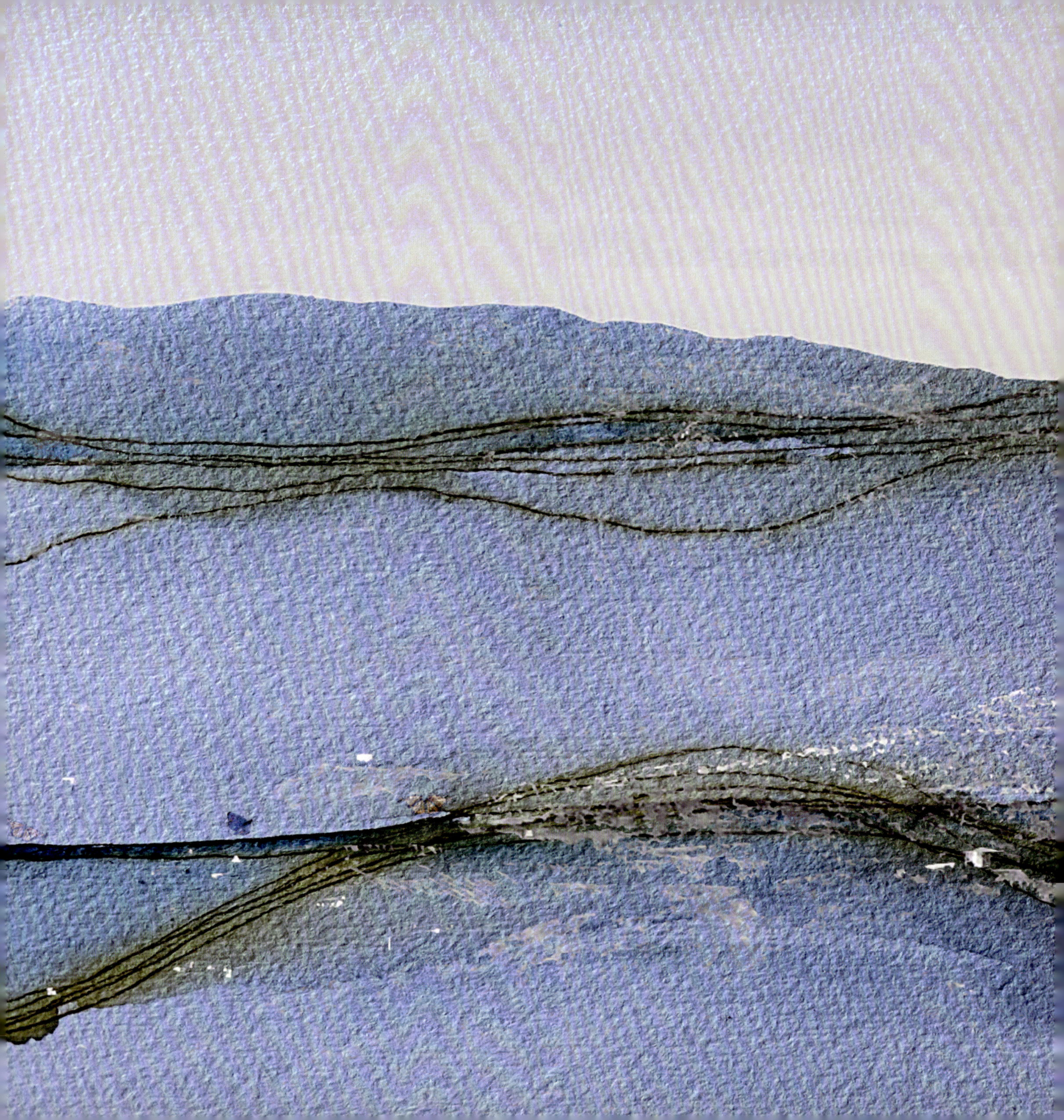

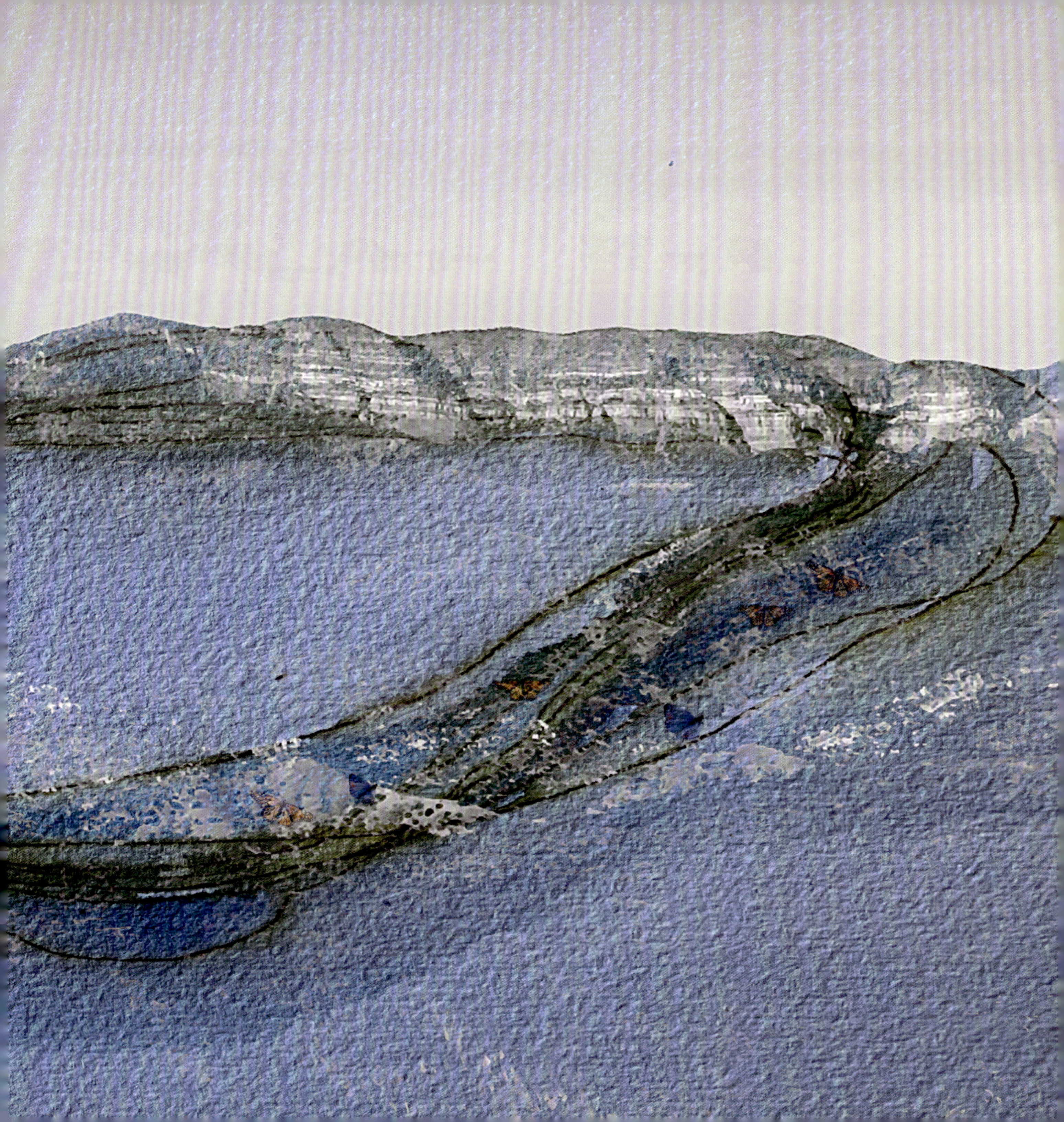

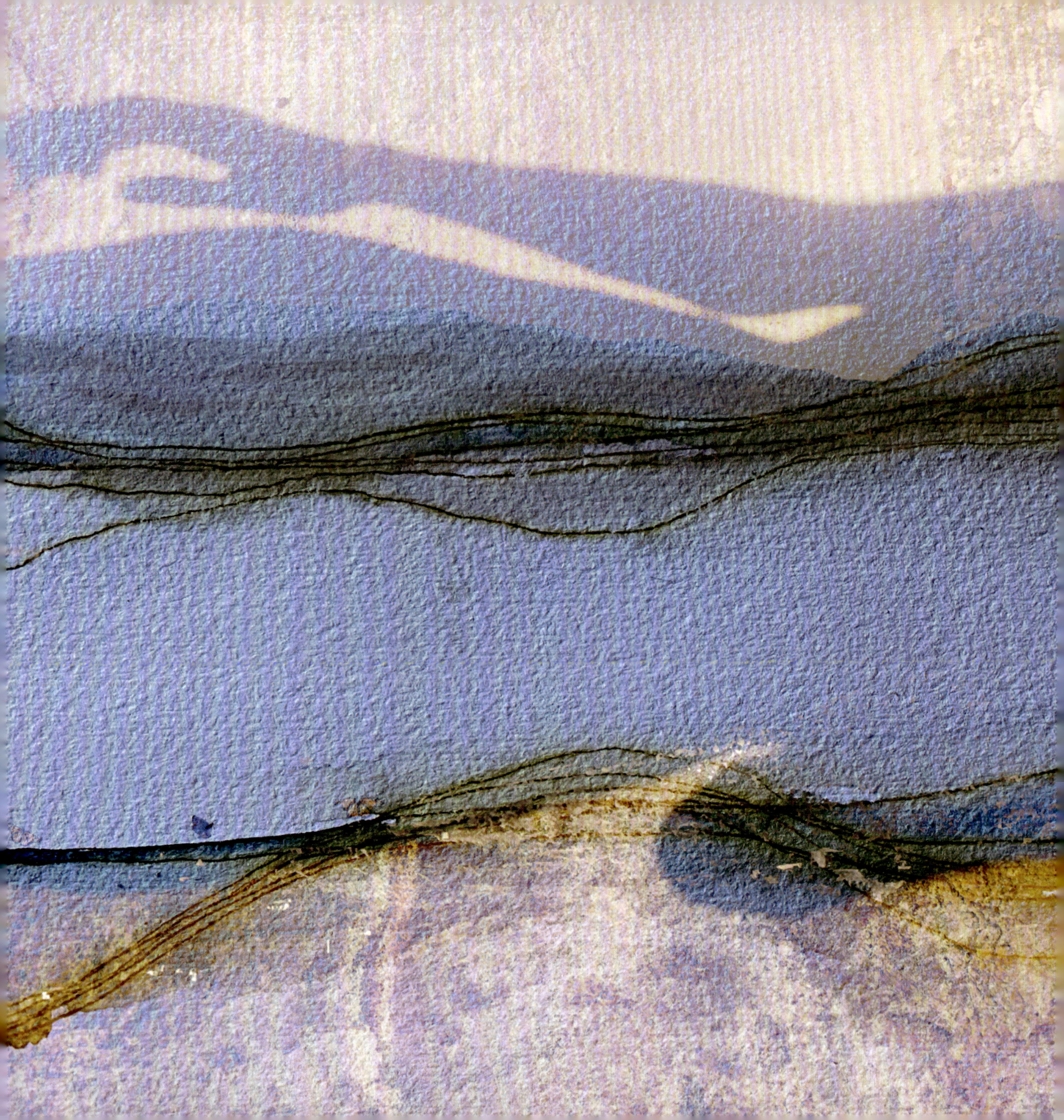

Can I write into the water
Does the water carry the story, the imprints of the land it moves through from sky to cloud to mountain valley and sea

Whispering the stories found in the earth quietly to the sky, lavishing the land with the opened heart of the clouds, falling and returning moving through roots, trunks, and leaves to go back up and continue the song, a very old song living in your body told in your sweat, circling through our sewers, out to the ocean, traveling up again, sharing the land with the sea with the sky again

always asking what world is at the center of your being

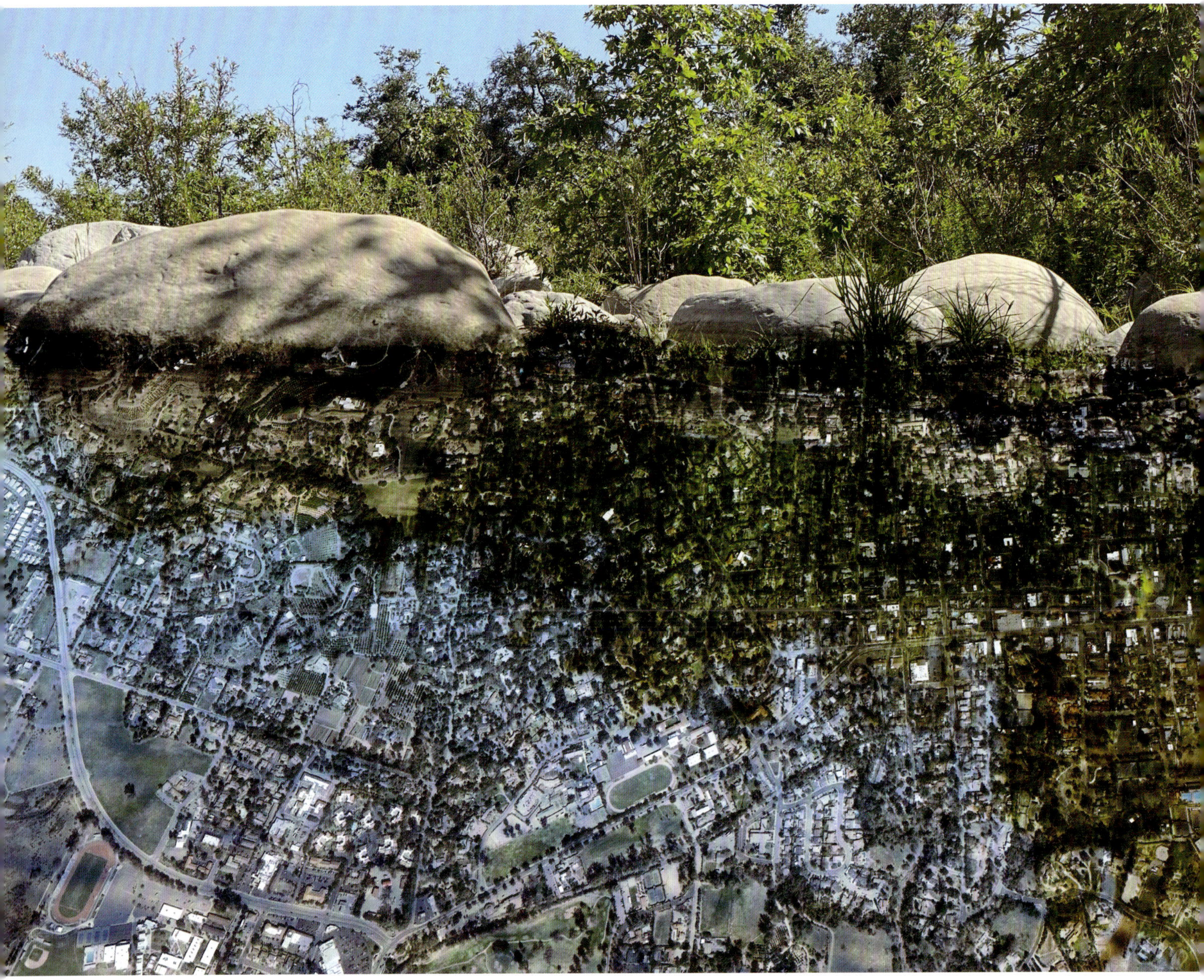

River inside the town

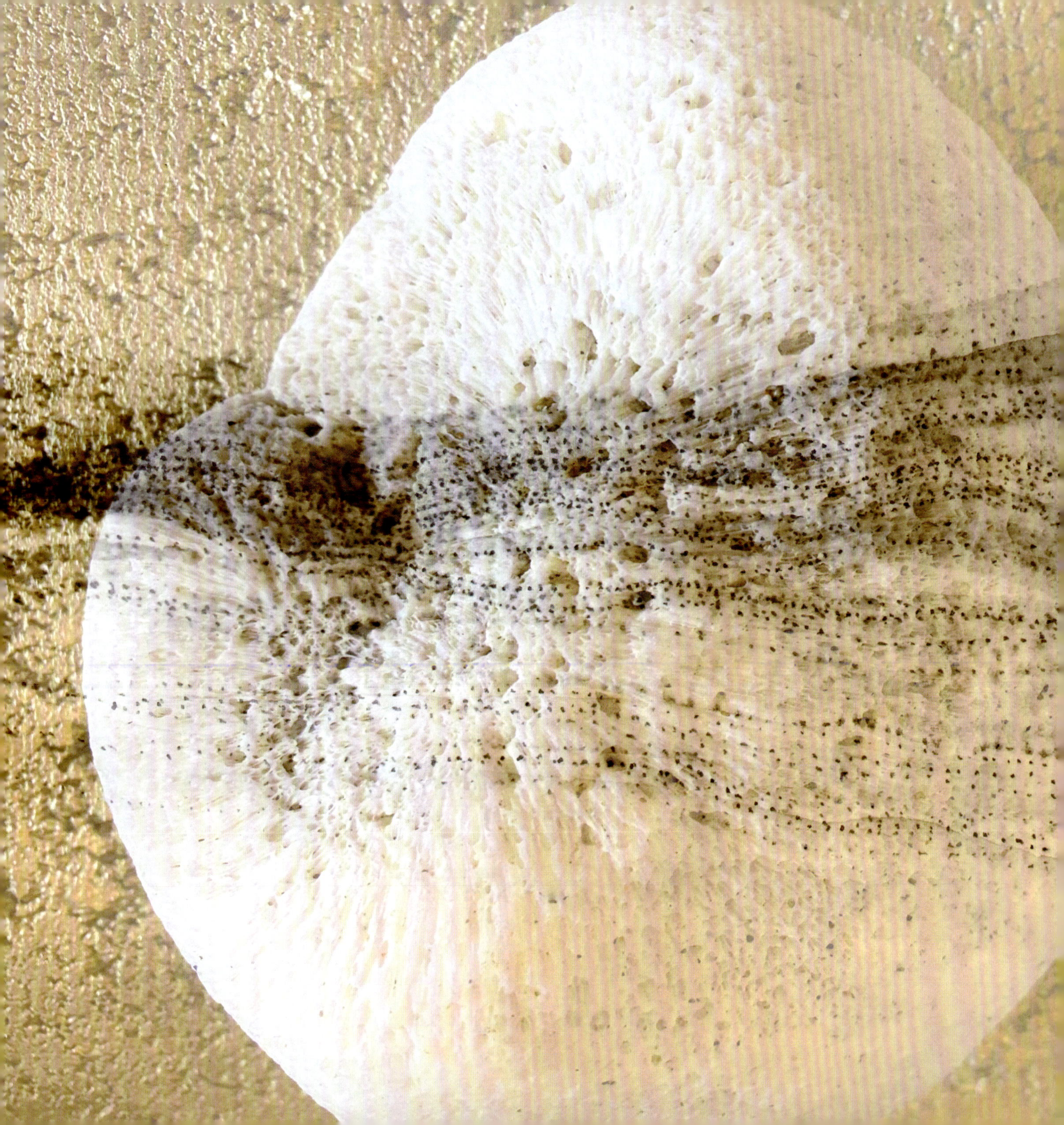

Feeling her gaze of pure joy hum inside me, and fill every cell, the joy of an entire sea, deep curiosity. Being in her gaze I want to enter the water forever, to be immersed in the flow of light and shadow. And then I am aware. There is a strange and beautiful sadness in being human. does she see it? Her freedom makes me feel the edges of my thoughts, like a tension I want to breathe in the gravity of the deep dark blue beneath her. I want to look into her eye for as long as she will allow, and the energy moving under my skin is difficult to hold, to stay with this feeling, it is a joy that seems familiar and like the human body no longer knows how to contain it. I am. The sea, the joy looking out through her, the salt everywhere.

but I keep reflexively resisting ever-expanding awe - and coming back to me - at the center, she is in the water and I am up here.

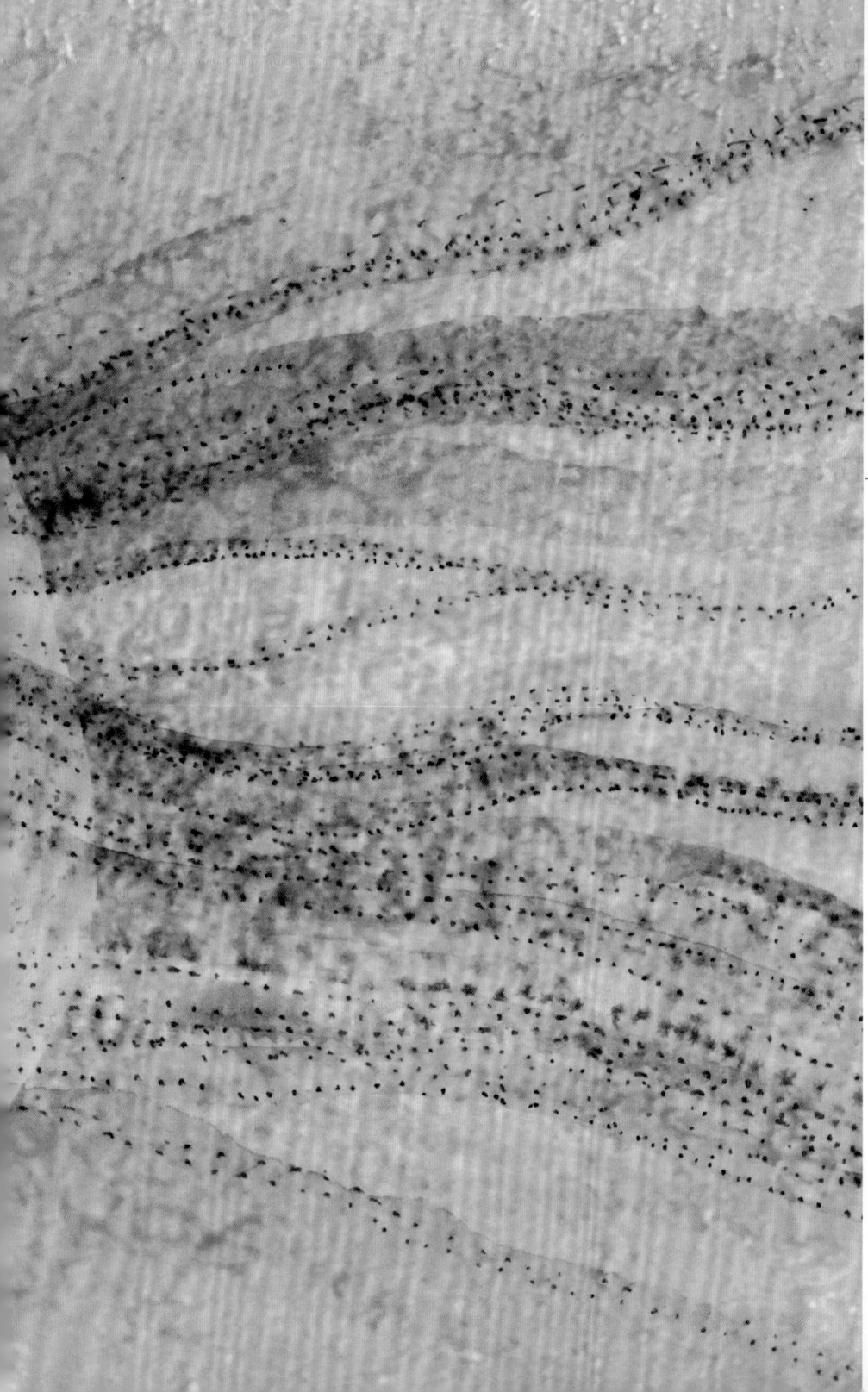

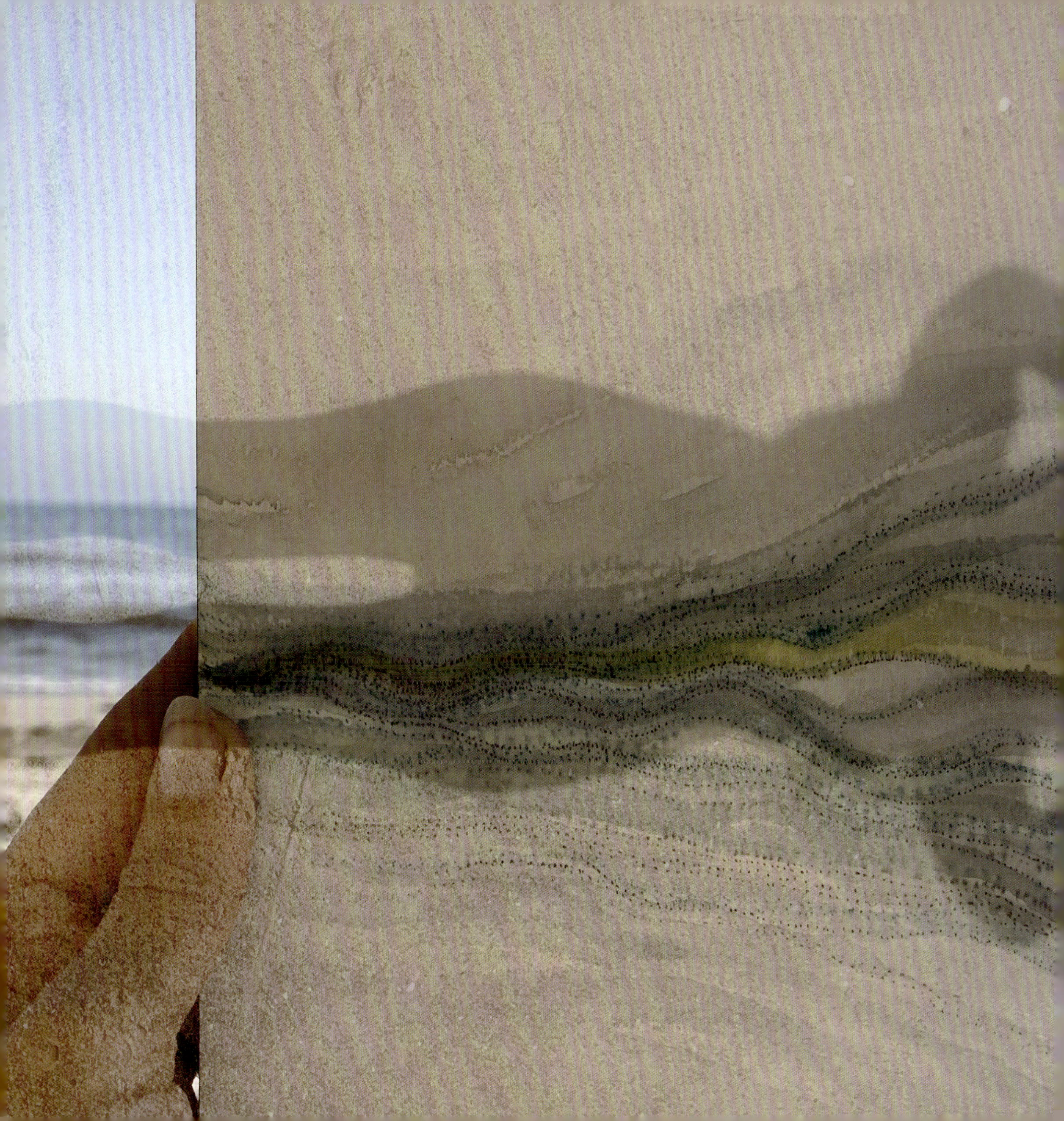

So much light refracted in every direction, a million shimmering beings

The boat breaks the surface of the sea speeding up and spraying light in all directions, falling back and dissolving into light. The panga captain who grew up on this vermillion sea and knows how to move with the pod of spinner dolphins at a speed that entices their playful nature. My father tells me to go to the front of the boat, so I lay at the bow with my head over the edge, the smooth skin of these creatures who are breathing air with me but returned to the water long ago is almost close enough to touch. The joy inside me explodes in sounds I don't recognize and can't control, and then the dolphin directly below me turns, swimming on her side effortlessly - looking up, into me. I am mirrored in the water below; she is mirrored in the sky above. Looking at her I don't know who I am, there is only almost unbearable joy

Sky and sea,
tree and roots,
mountain and valley.
Every time I really remember and hold her gaze inside, like I am remembering now, my eyes fill with salty water again

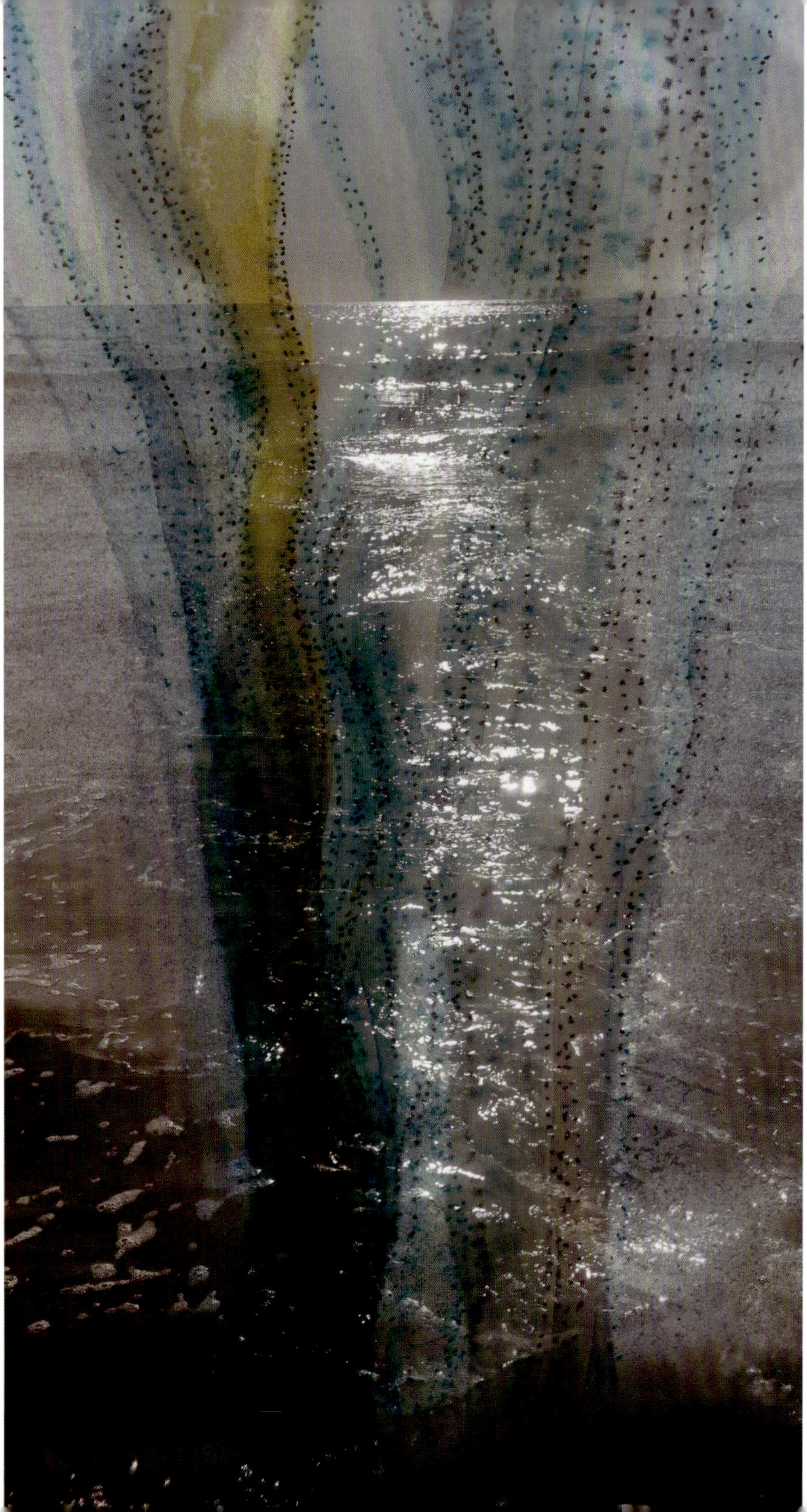

The dark sea inside my body, moving down towards the earth there is no bottom, no floor,
moving up towards the sky the density of blue opens, allowing light in
So much light refracted in every direction, a million shimmering beings
Looking at her I don't know who I am, there is only almost unbearable joy

Sky and sea,
tree and roots,
mountain and valley.

Can I write into the water
sharing the land with the sea with the sky again

always asking what world is at the center of your being

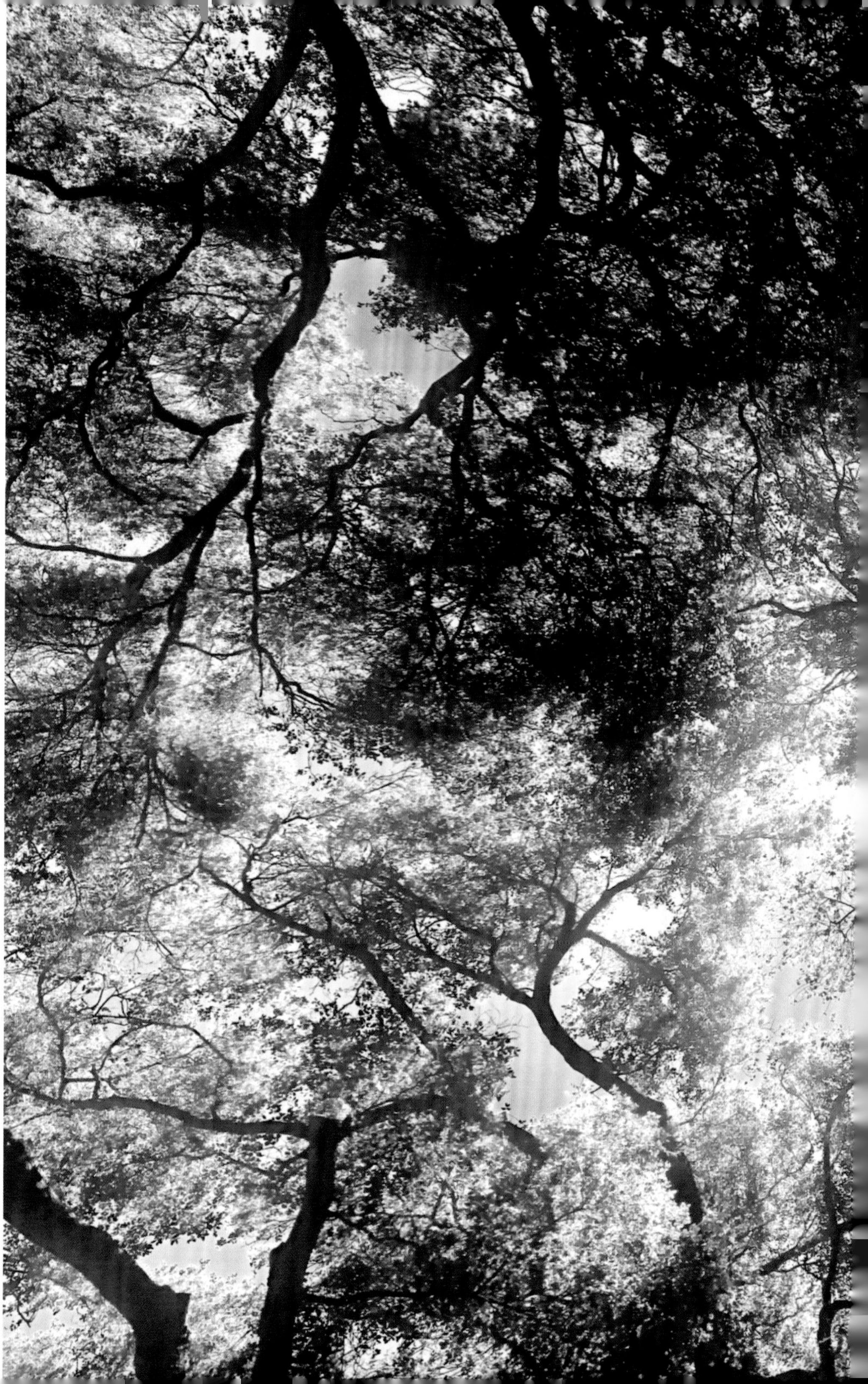

under the sea

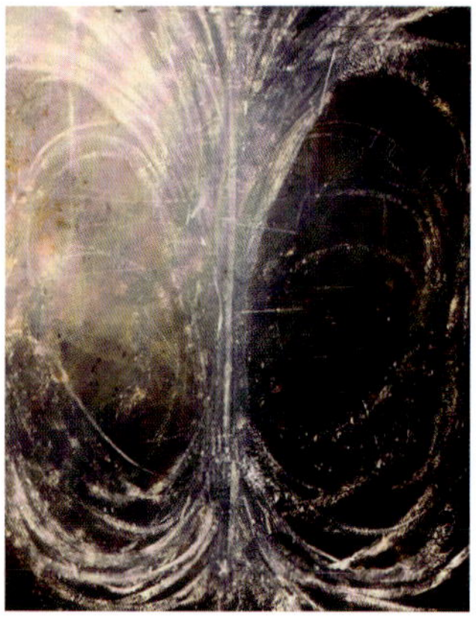

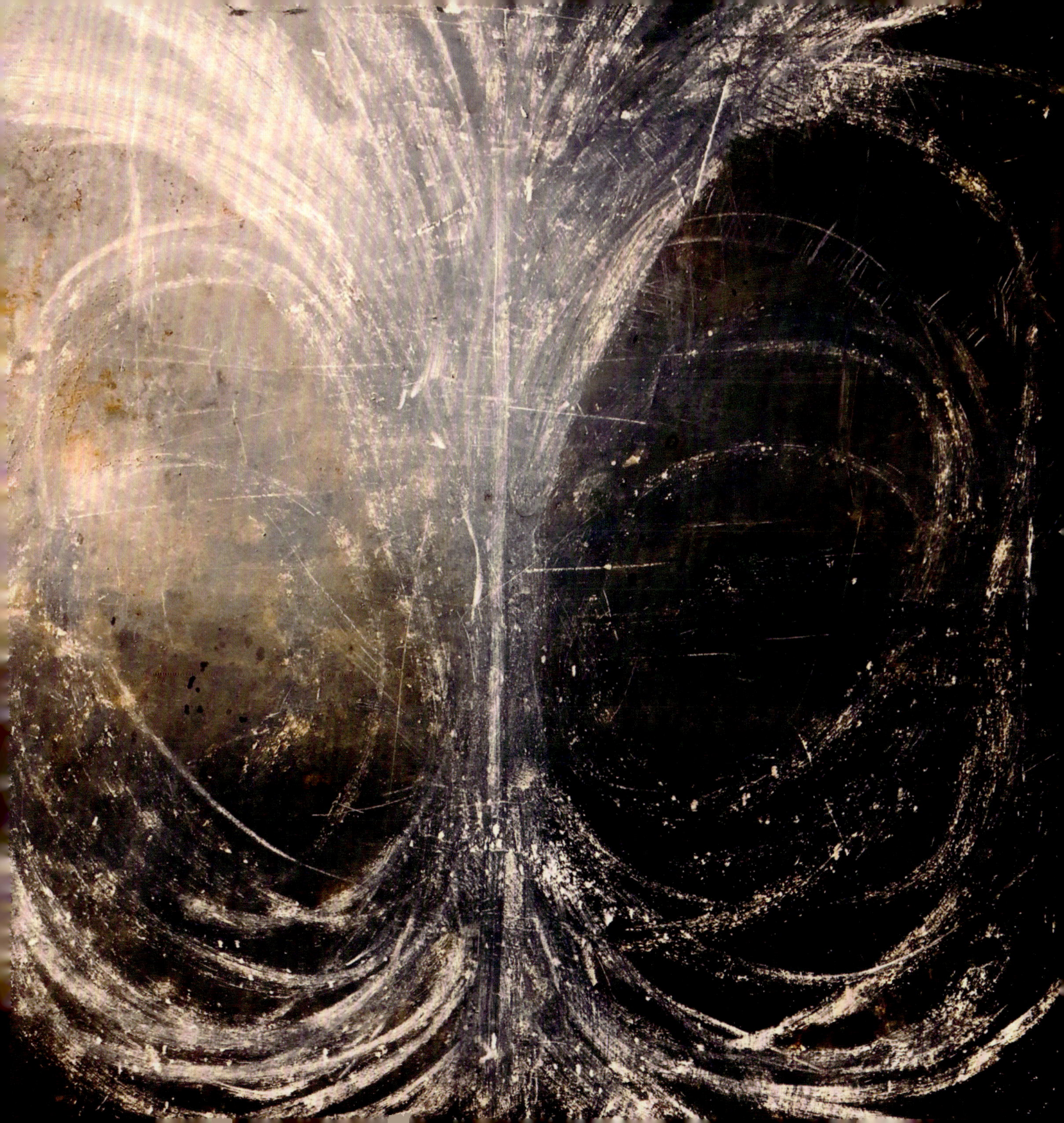

Sky 2

# *What would happen…*

…if movement were seen as most basic and the default state of the world, and stillness as the exception? And isn't the former actually more true to life than the latter?

Take a simple plant. It might be stationary, but isn't it constantly in motion? The movement of water and nutrients, the bending and the resilience to wind and other forces of nature, all is an incessant process that will continue even after the plant dies. The stems and leaves appear to have certain resting points relative to the wind blowing over them. There are probably mathematical models that affirm this, but that is beside the point. There is a rhythm to it all, a rhythm that can be felt and understood by being present on the land, in the field, with the plants, with the creatures great and small, with the elements.

Watching the wind blow over a field of grass or other vegetation, and keeping one's attention on the recurrent gusts of wind generating a glistening motif running across the bending plants, can instigate elation and inner calm. Sunlight being reflected on a water surface can be equally nourishing, rousing the wavy nature we all carry.

One way to visually allude to the continuous flux in nature is to take the elements in view that are moving as primary. Then, to shift away from photo-realism and linear perspective, without the depictions losing veracity—it still has to feel real. Close approximations of this in print, digital, or other media are comic art, some twentieth-century art movements (such as futurism), Japanese woodblock prints, and various indigenous artistic styles.

This proposal of the "moving-life" as opposed to "still-life" drawing and painting can be both challenging on a personal level and on the cultural level. In most art schools—implicit but present—one is taught to focus on the static view. The depiction of movement is usually reserved for animation and "low-brow" art, without any reflection on why this is so.

Of course video art can also give a taste of nature's flux, but usually some distance gets infused as a consequence of the lenses used to film the movement. And this leaves very little to the imagination…

*On hot summer evenings, the swallows are flying over in great numbers. Their dance is erratic yet beautiful, with a certain order to it that I cannot fully grasp. I know they are moving like this to catch insects as quick as they can, but that changes very little my sense of bewilderment. These birds do not know the secret to their exquisite choreography, and nor do I…*

49

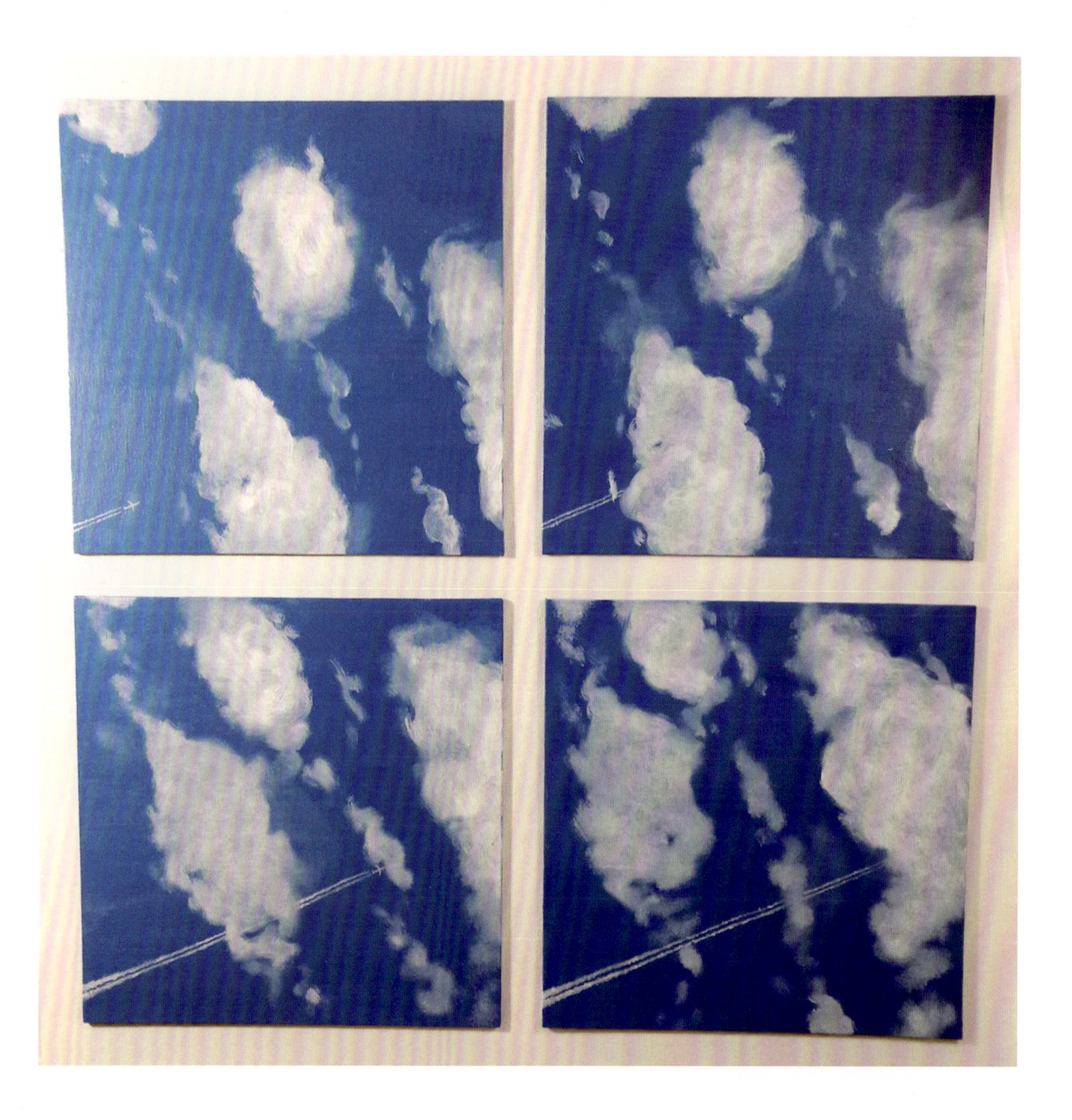

# Letters of Philosophy

Maria Hvidbak

Hit me. Breathe, the sweet smell of
a fifty-six-year-old preowned piece of
mechanics. Absorb the rhythmic sounds of my
heavy weight body translating your temper
of the moment into shades of black on white.
Participate, with whatever meaning will
then be growing on the paper before you.
  -Olympia SM9 De Luxe

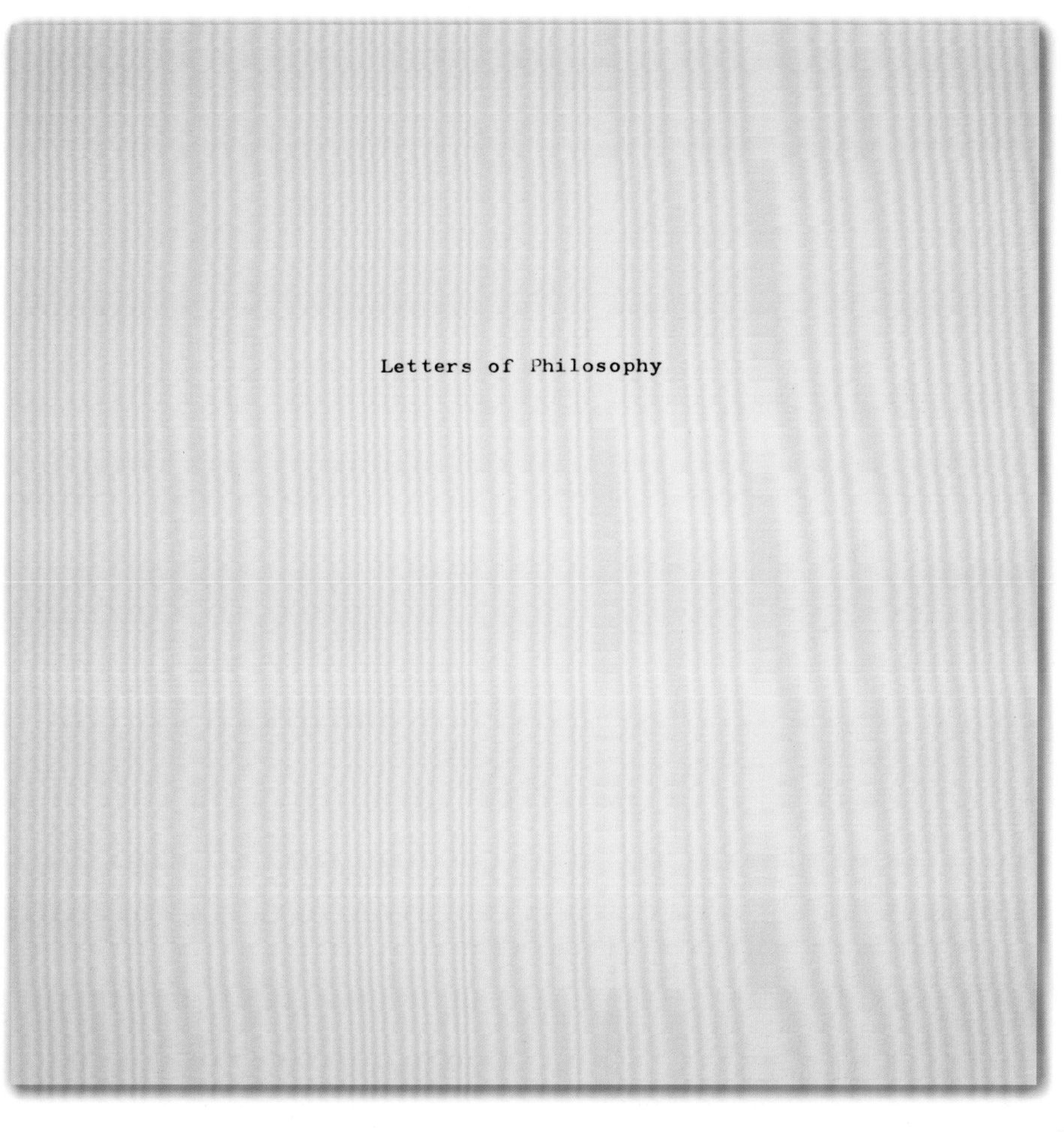

Letters of Philosophy

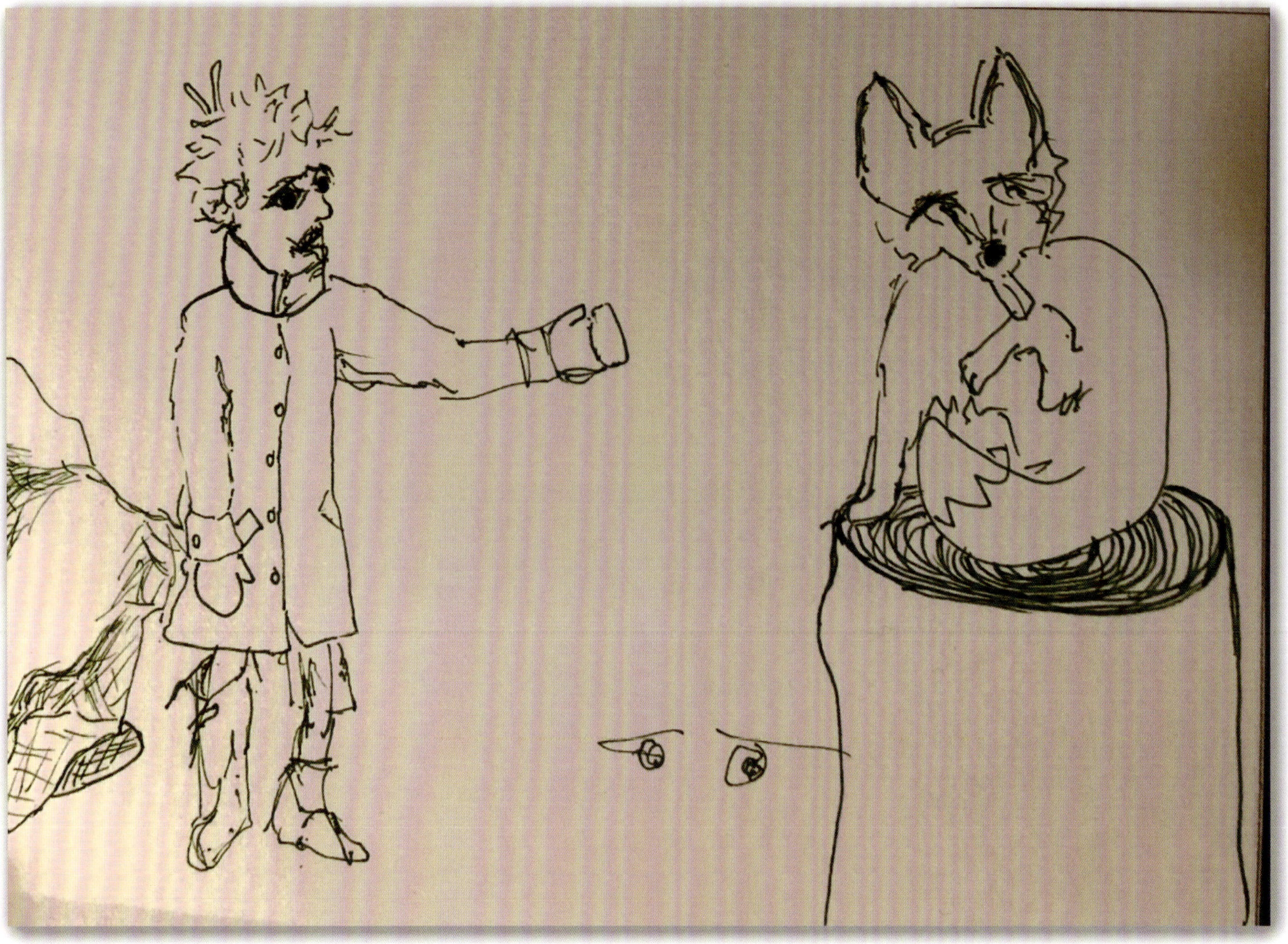

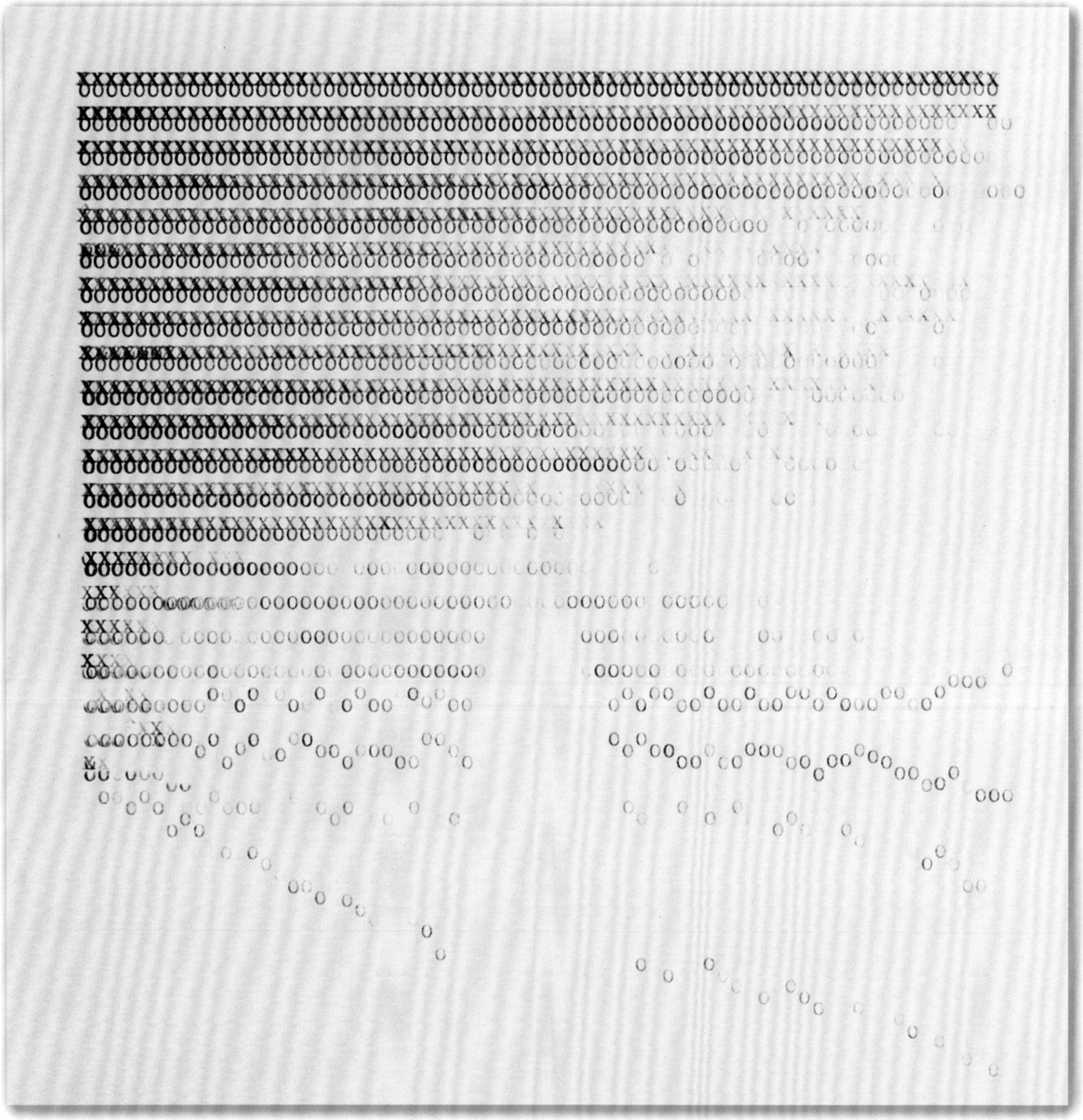

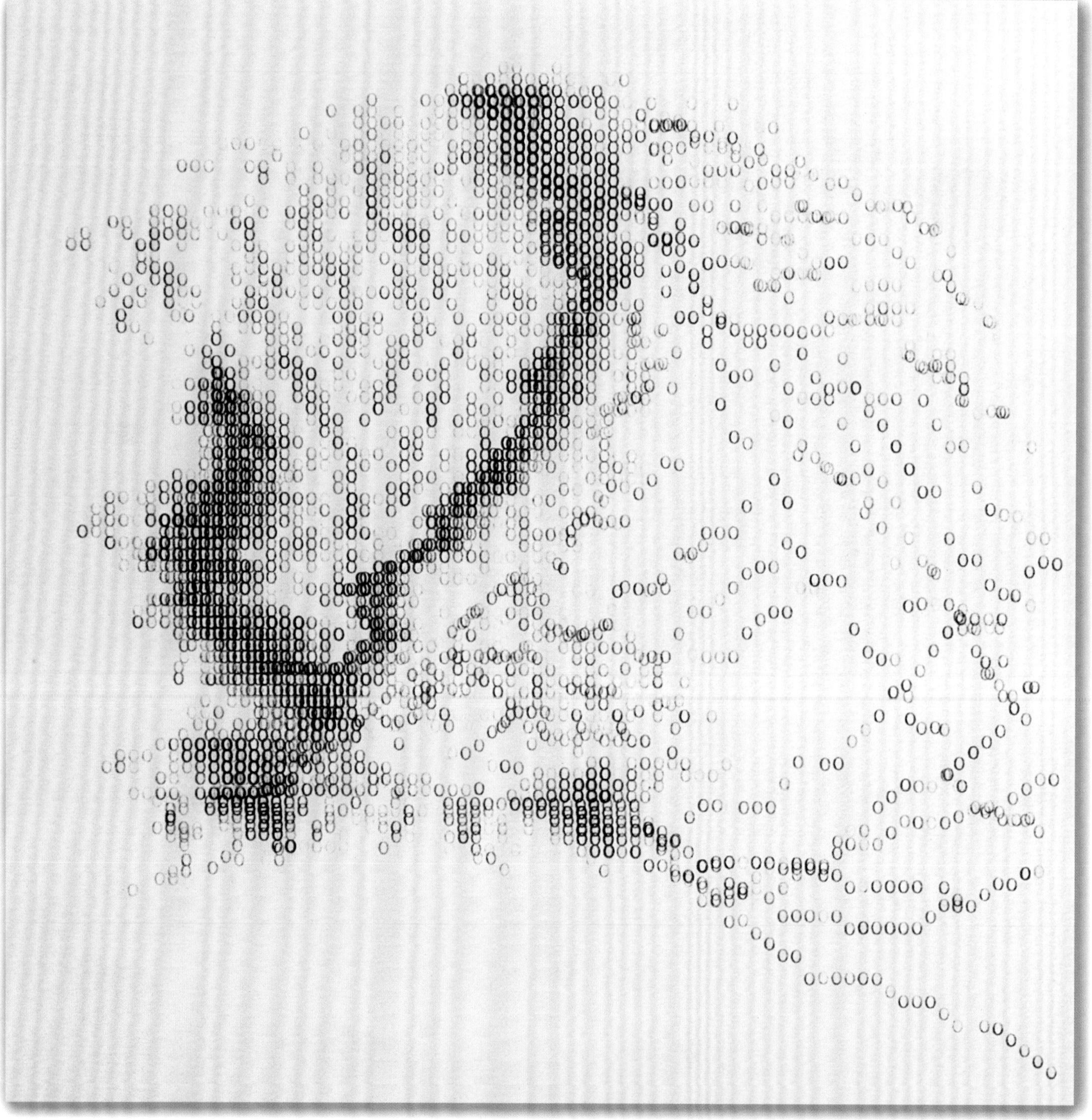

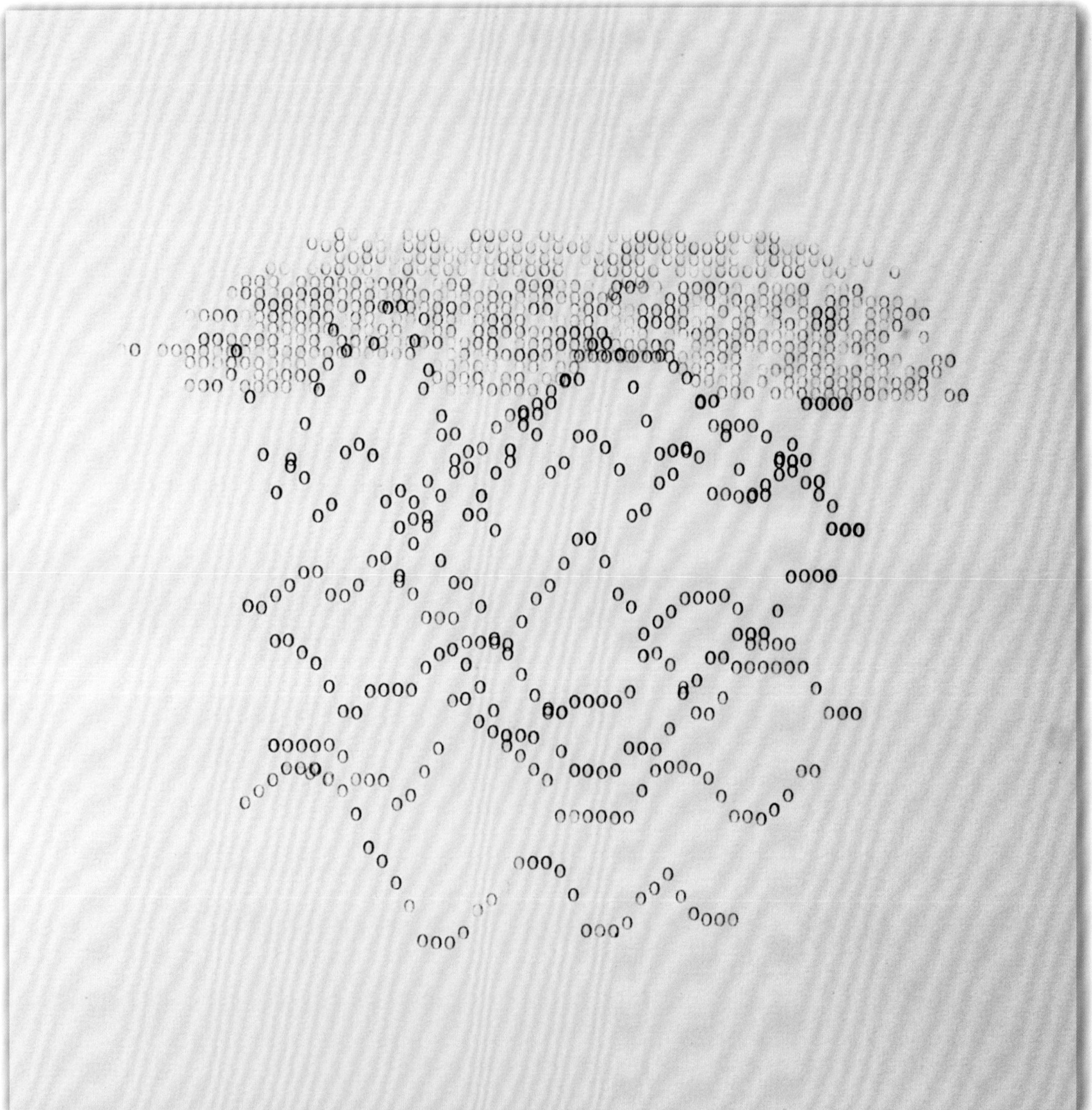

60

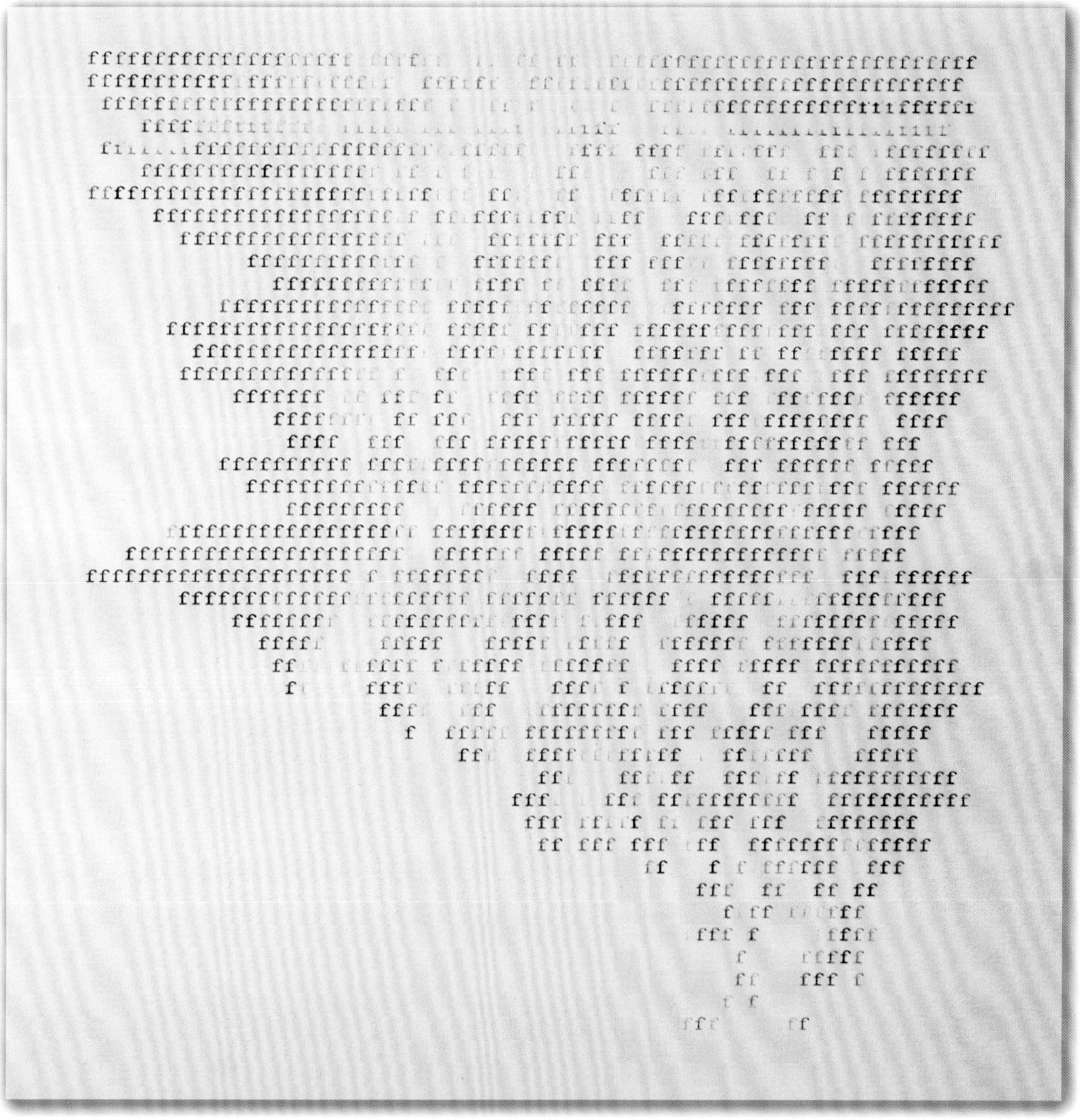

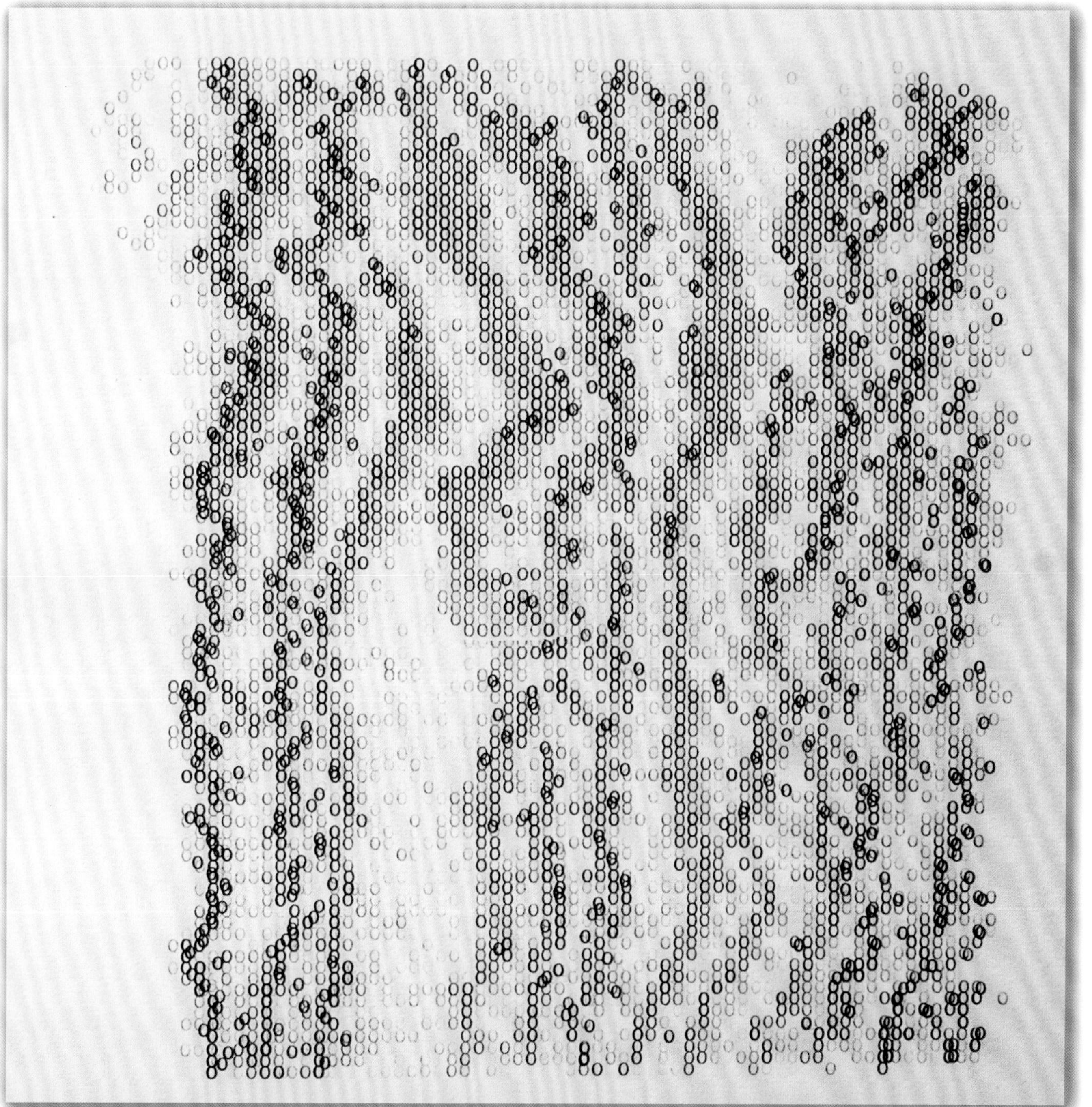

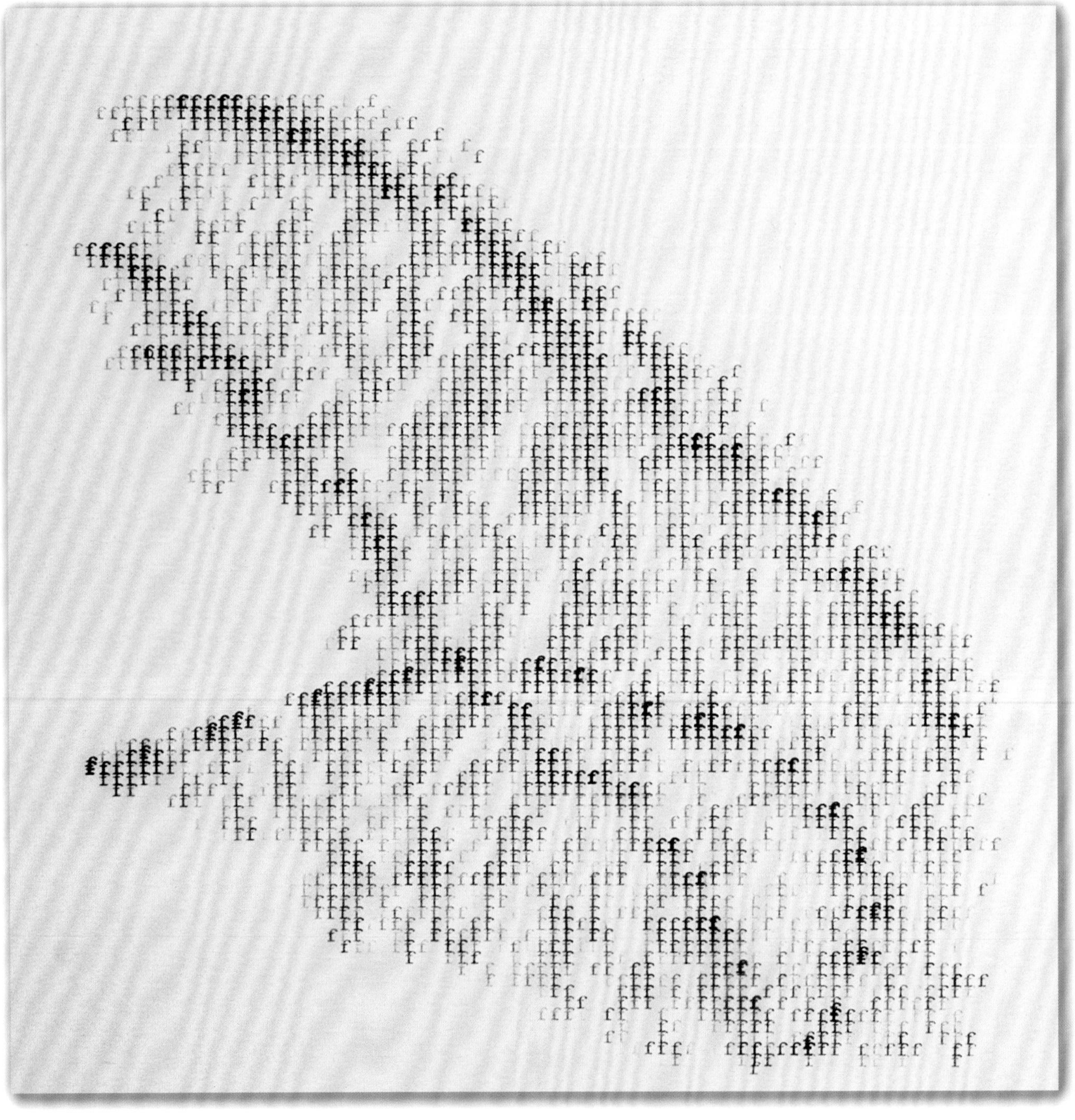

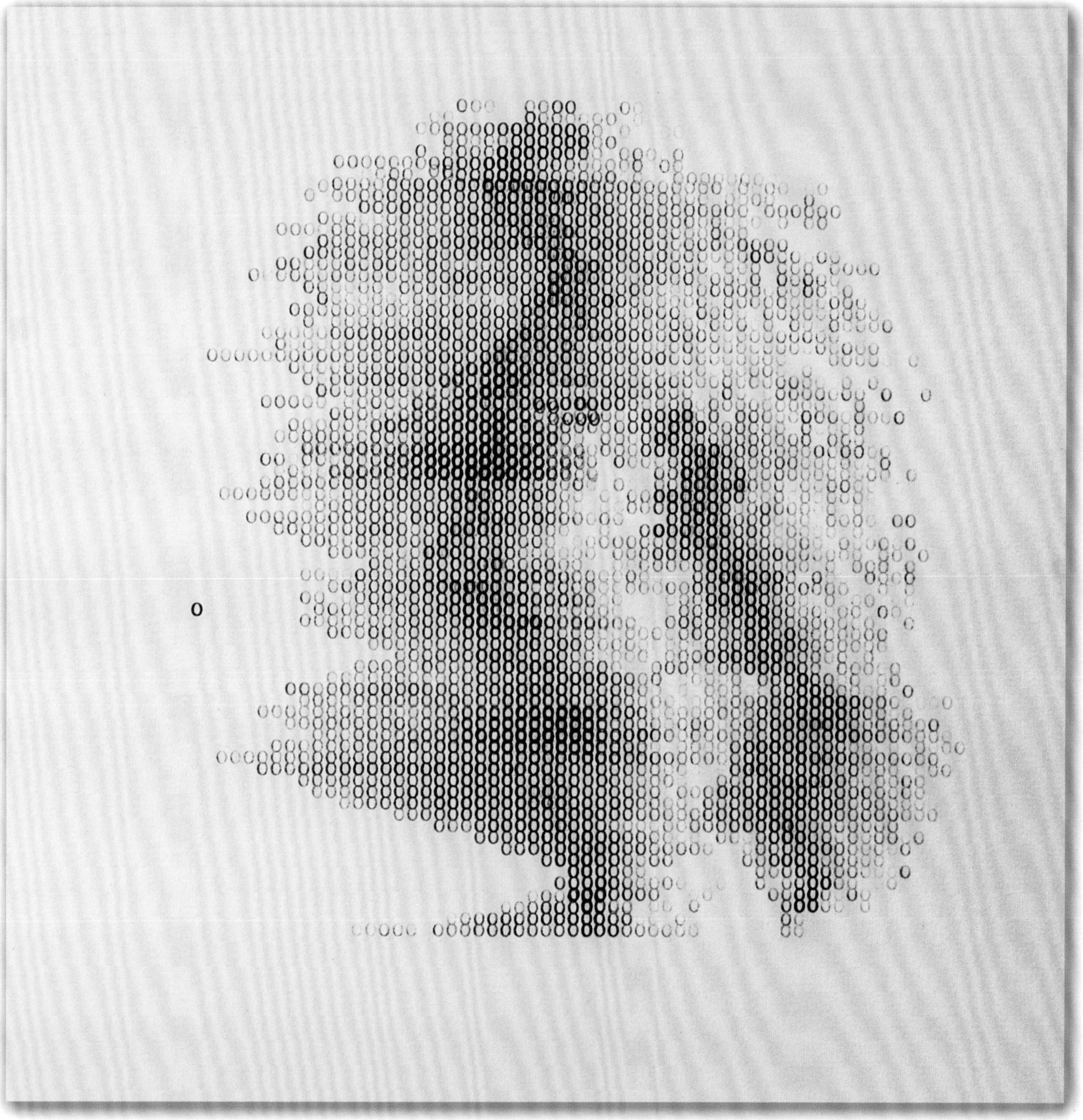

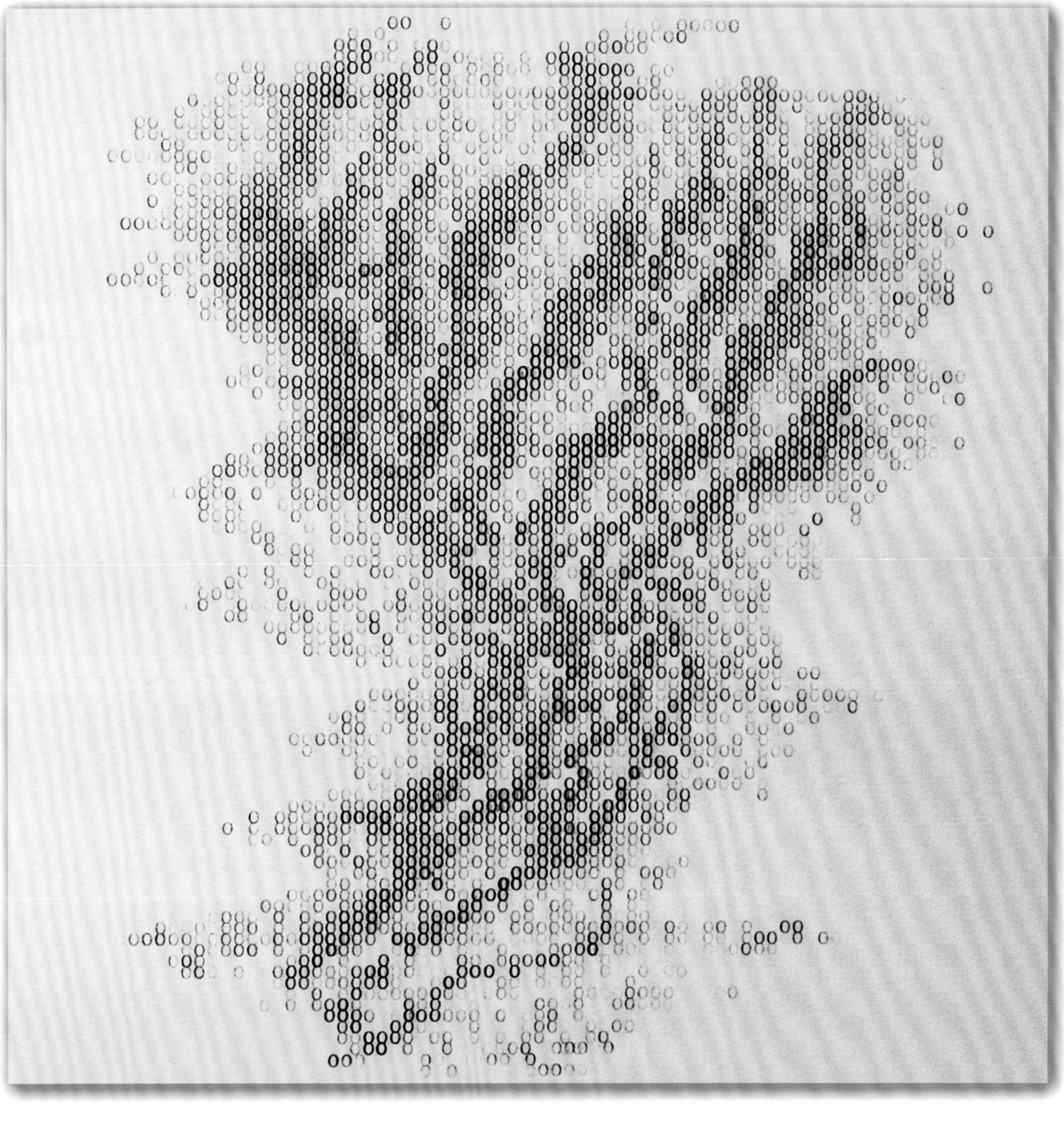

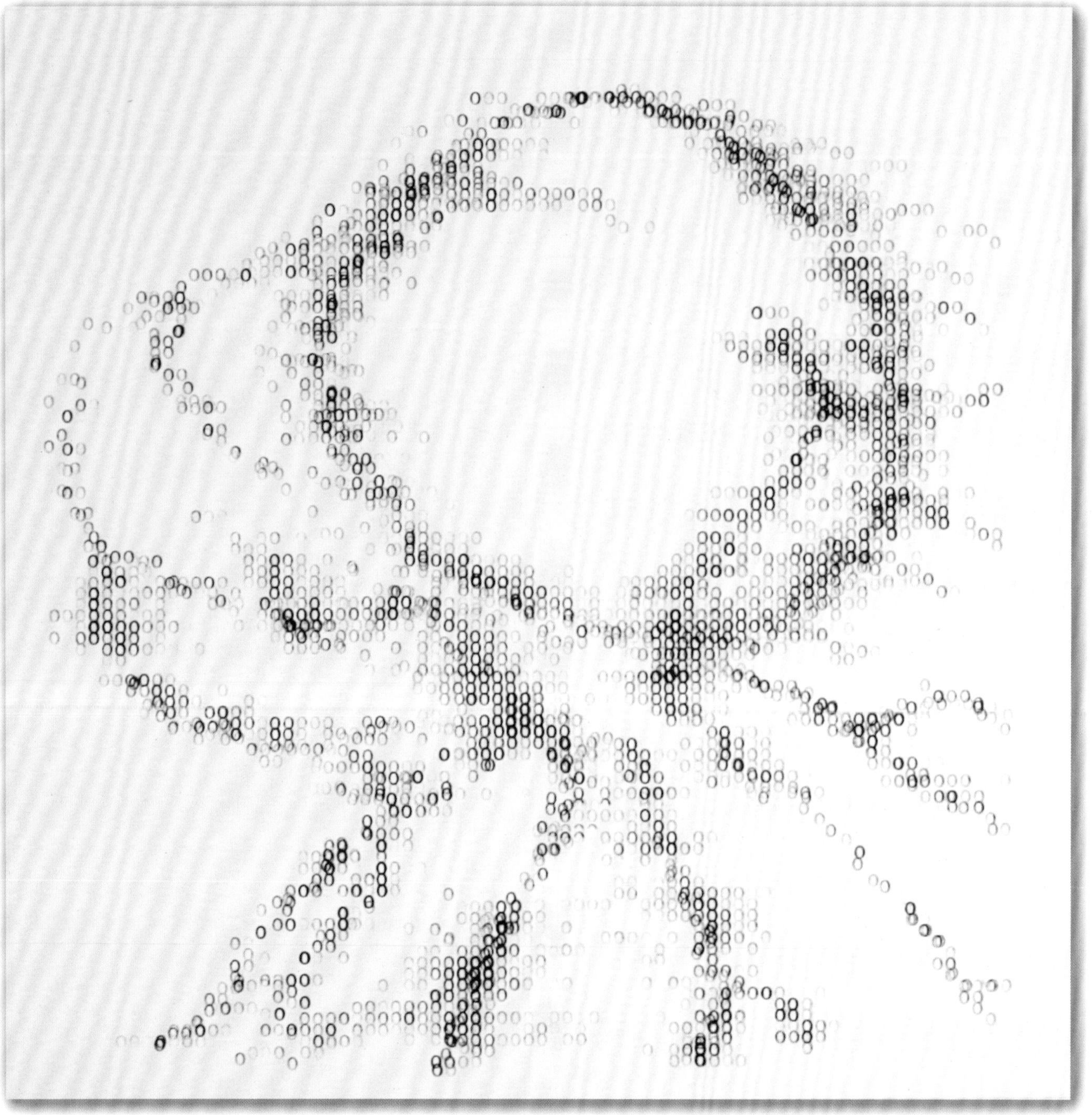

69

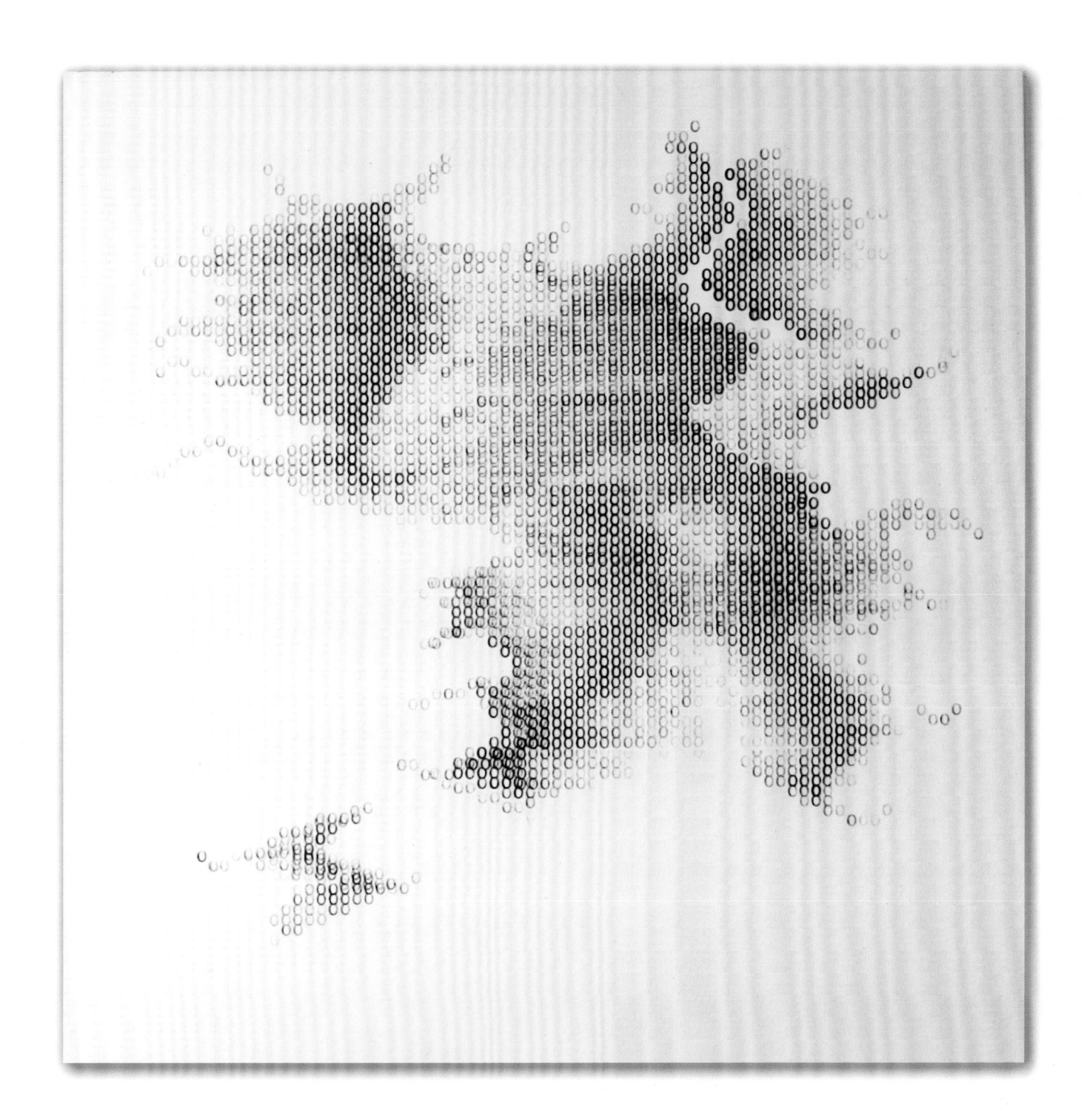

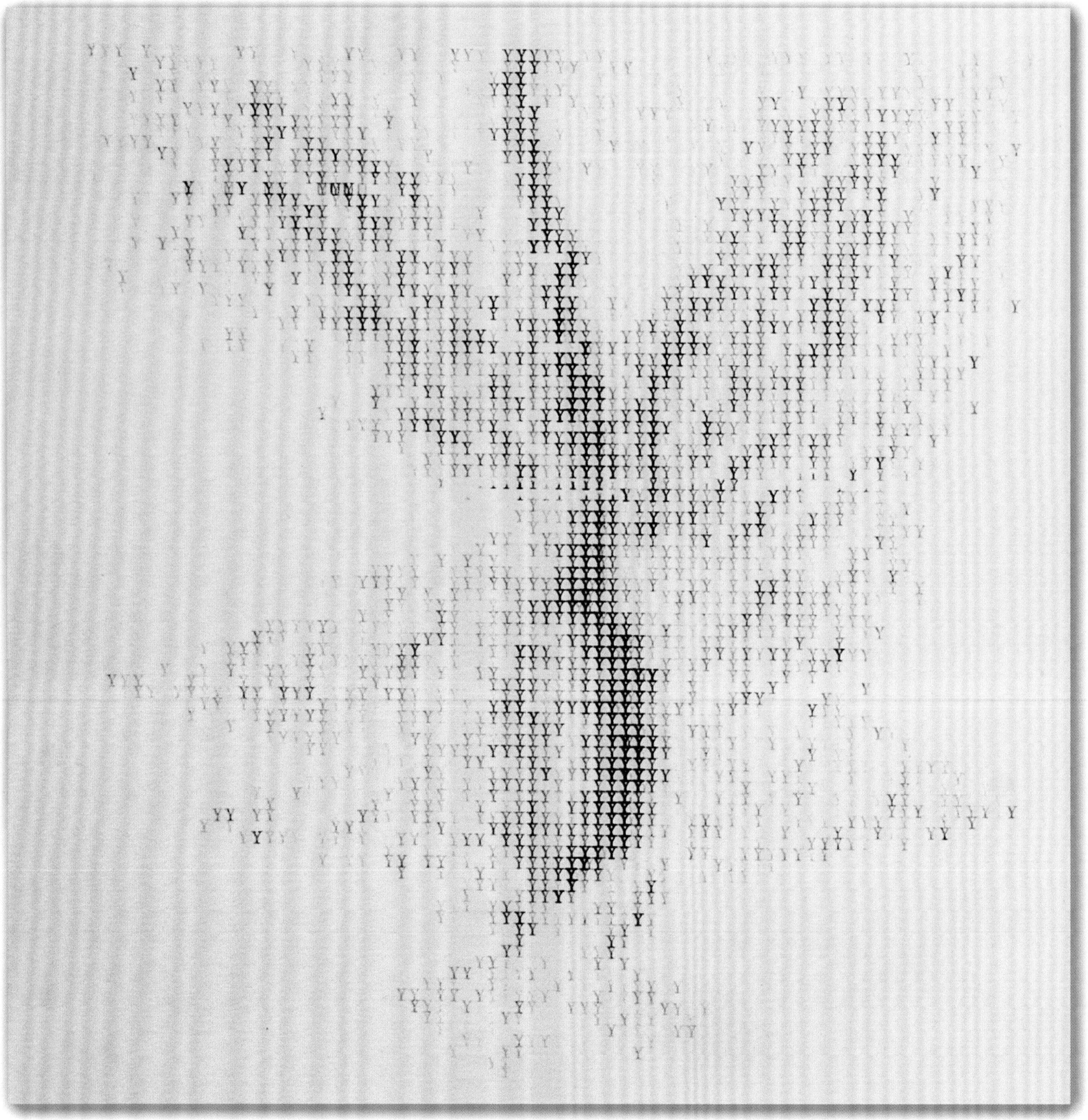

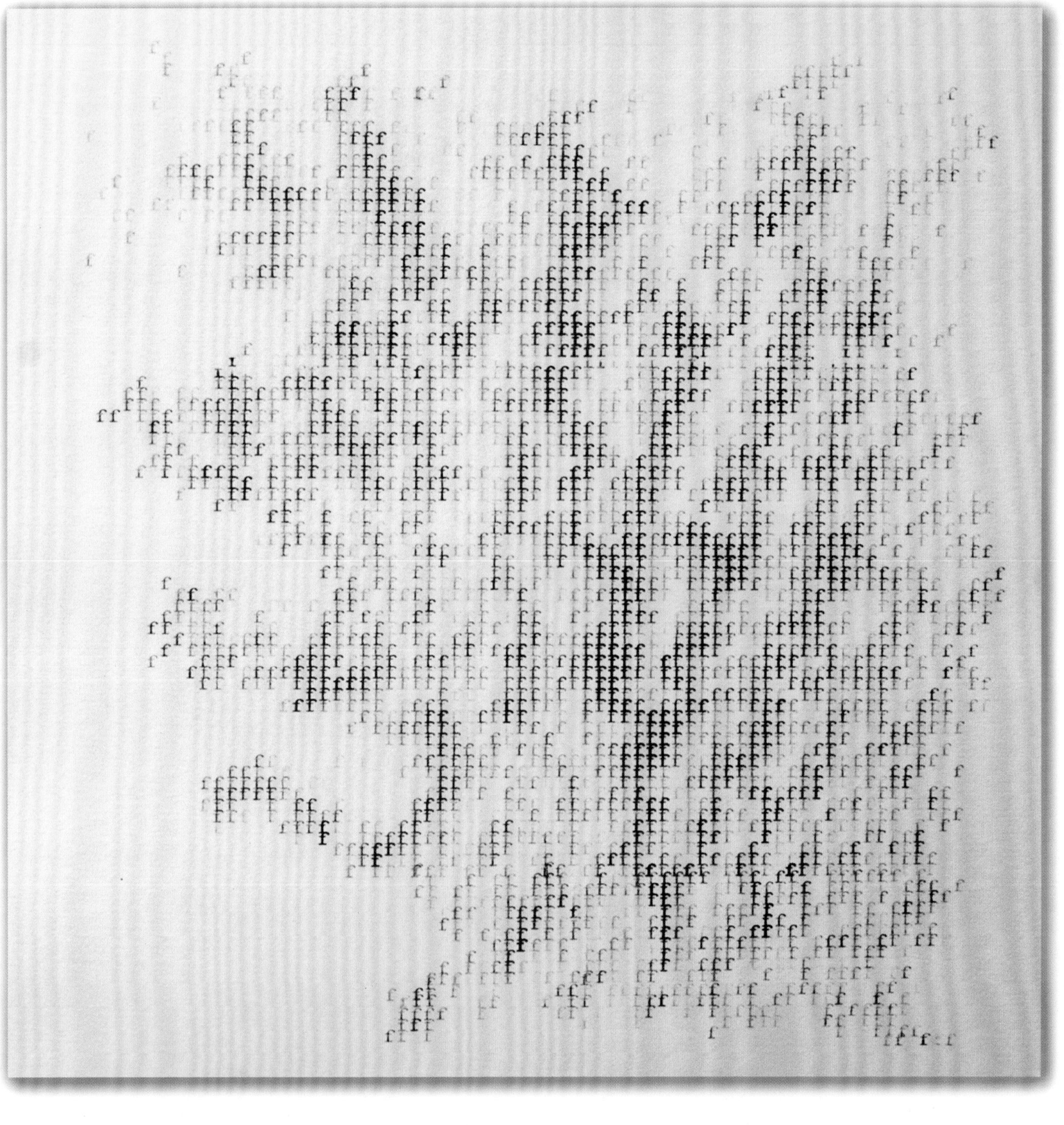

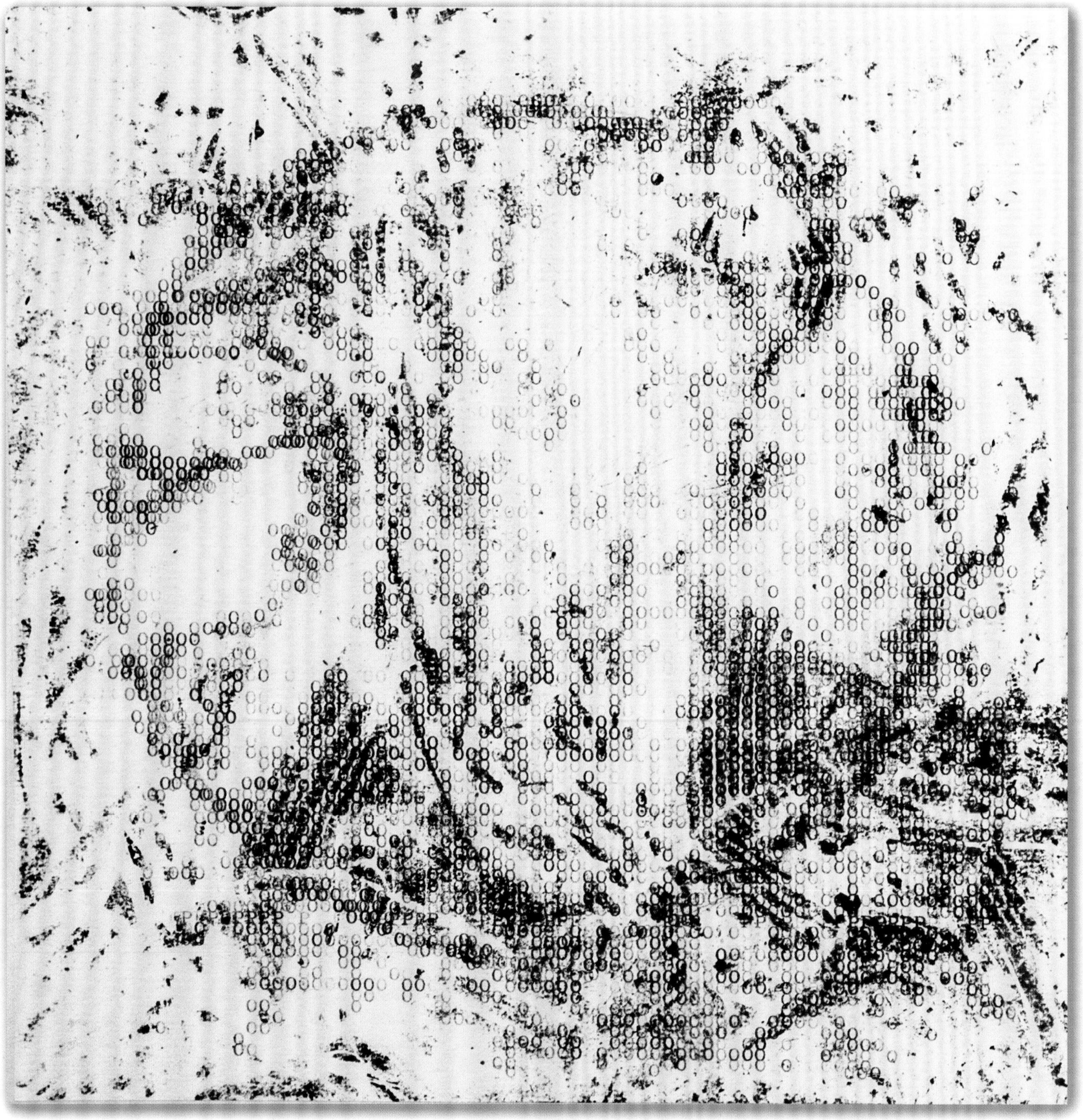

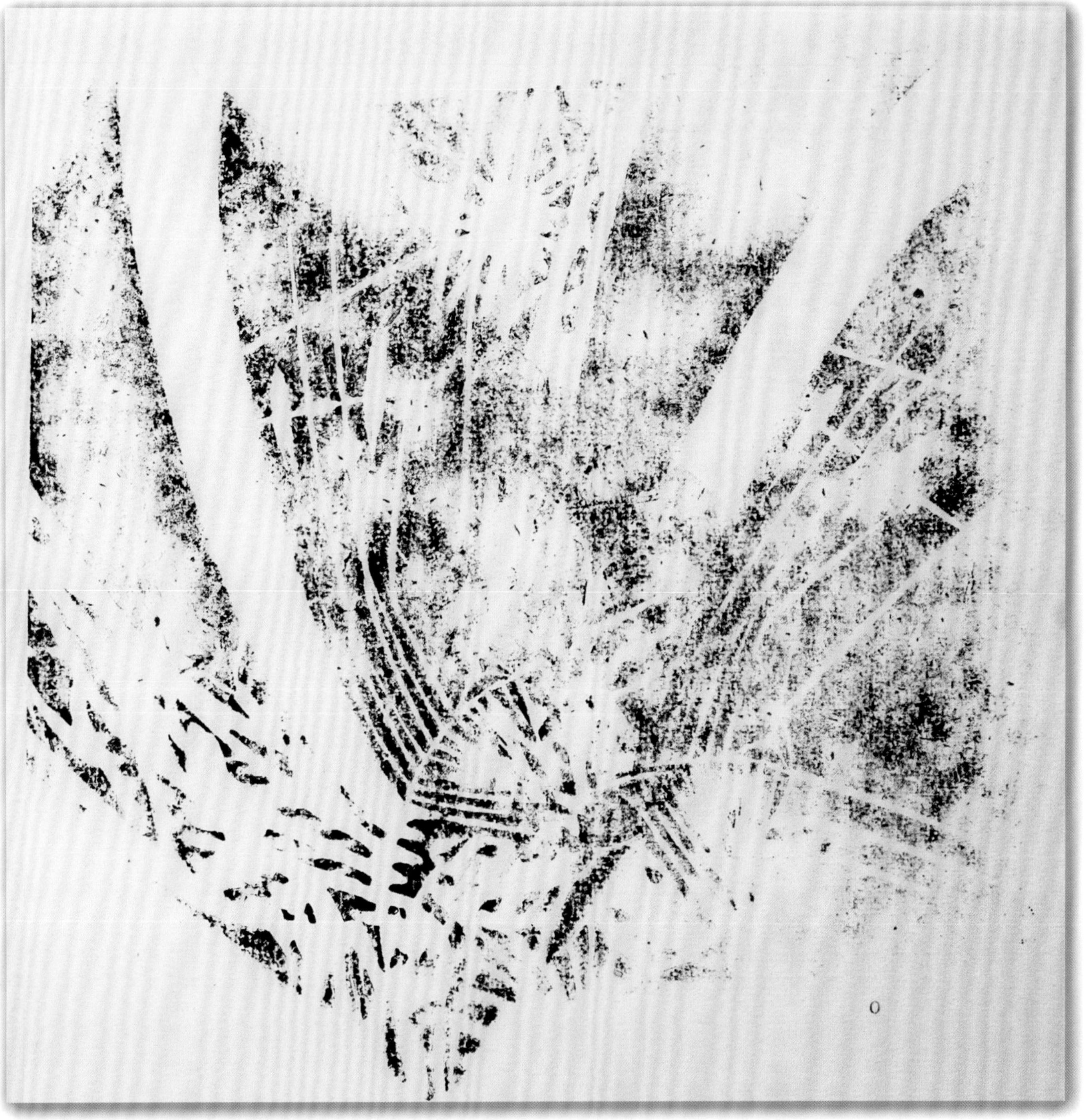

75

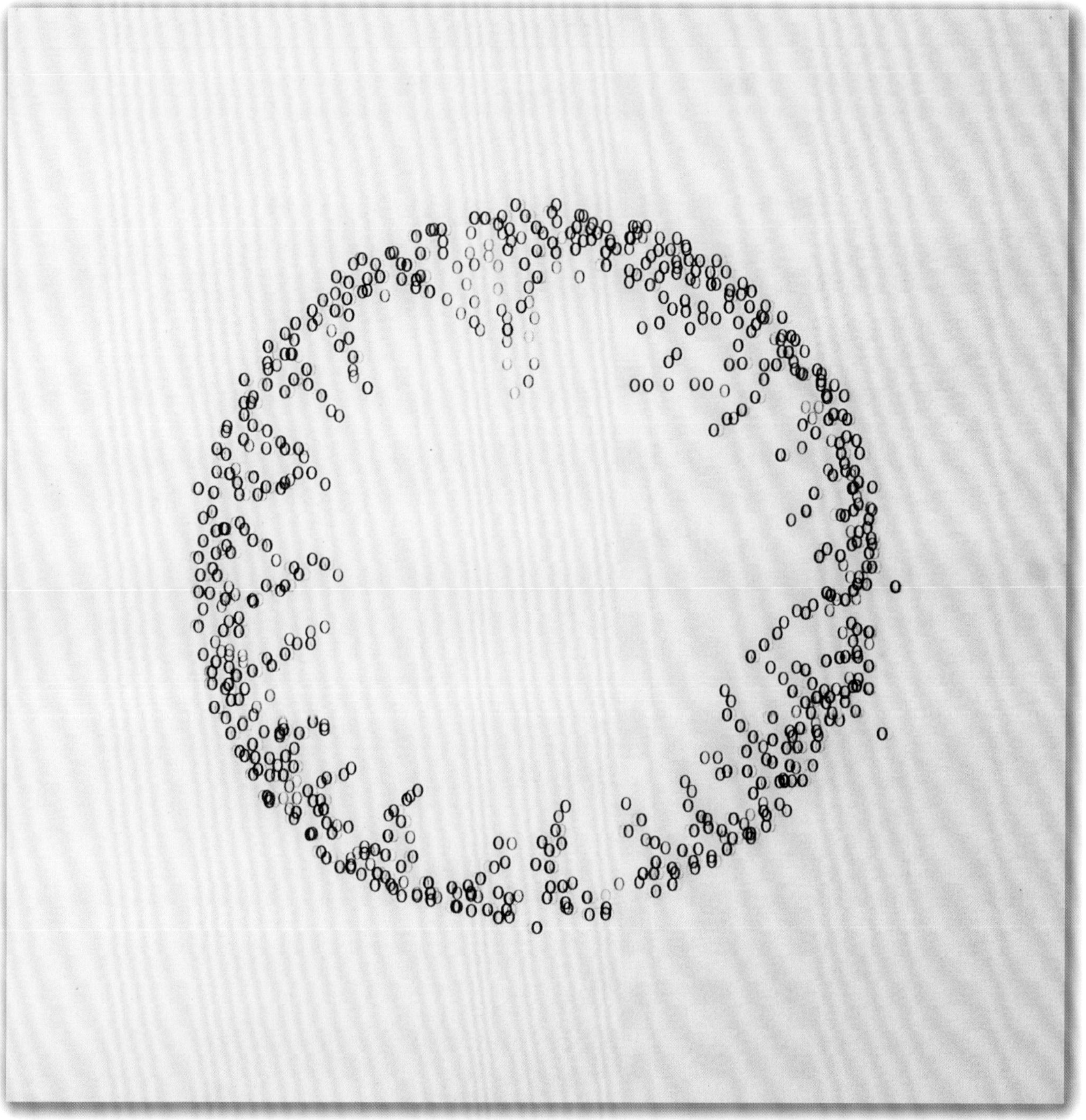

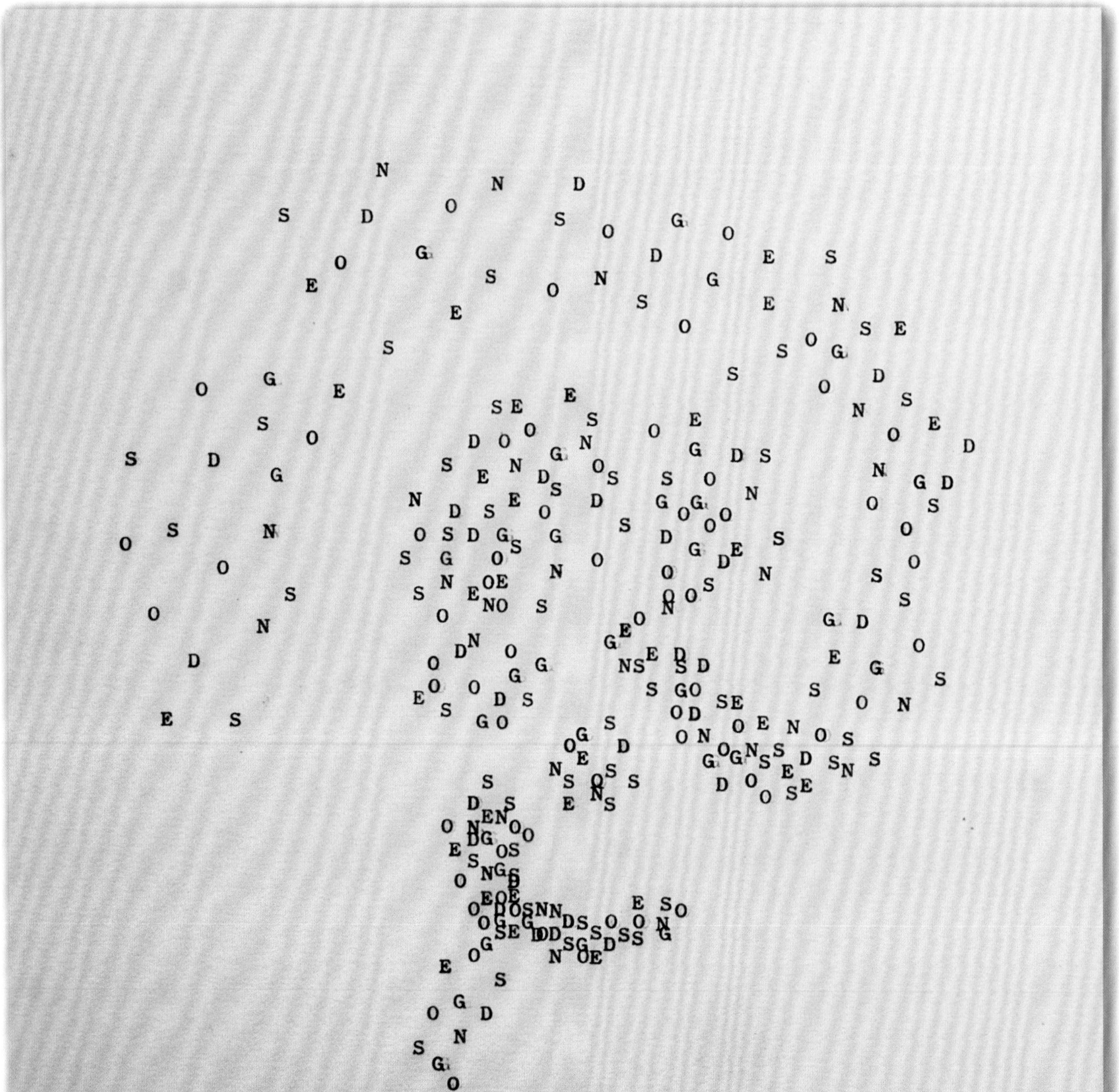

The girl, on her daily walk to nowhere, suddenly bumped into a red fox; And, since it was a talking fox, the girl took the opportunity to start a conversation with the fox.

"I'd rather not bore you with clever words" she began.
"Please feel free not to do so" said fox.

The
Beginning

Sky 3

## *Technology at every step…*

…from shoes to roads to lenses to computers, has enabled us to *transcend* nature and create more distance. Perhaps it is now time to *inscend*, to change course and step back *into* nature. A world in flux is natural, ubiquitous, common. A static picture is unnatural, a statistical anomaly. We tend to believe and hold to the contrary. So many things are considered normal and taken for granted!

Reality can be said to be a form of hypnosis, of "make-believe" in the images and stories constructed and shared. Some go so far as to think of reality as a shared hallucination or a consensus-based trance. Photography in this day and age is very much a part of this persistent illusion that is widely accepted as true and objective.

A camera usually registers the reflection of light on the surfaces of objects within the picture frame, in a moment of time. Because of this feat, David Hockney mockingly calls the camera the "paralyzed cyclops." That is not to say that photography cannot sometimes transcend its basic shortcomings. The medium does have its merits and possibilities. However, photographic and photo-like images provide only a limited view of the world that cannot make up for the visual richness and freedom that is possible with fully embodied observation in real time.

As a consequence of this, the order within a photograph is rather limited compared to that of a rich painting or drawing. The awareness and imagination of the visual artist enable more possibilities to emerge in the perception of the viewer.

There is little doubt that a significant part of our consciousness is shaped by the thousands, if not millions of images we have digested since birth, via magazines, television, all sorts of books, the internet, etc. This begs the question of the extent to which our imagination and our assumptions about reality are formed by photography.

It might seem straightforward, but we easily forget that our eyesight is elliptical, not rectangular. It is only because of technical limitations and practical reasons that photographs and screens are almost always rectangles. Our vision, on the other hand, is sharp and focused in the center and gets blurry as you move away from the center. Physically, it is all cones, ellipses and ellipsoids that make up the vision process, no rectangular shapes to be found anywhere! This is just one insight of many one can have when examining the effects of living with screens and products of photography on human consciousness.

*When they are born, the vision of babies is blurred. For some time, there is very little differentiation going on, without boundaries between the baby and her environment. The body, including the brain, needs to learn a great deal to become a semi-autonomous organism, eventually establishing invariant features in the visual field. As the infant grows older, lenses and other devices resolve the blurriness and enable us to look much further, and to observe a lot more detail. But what gets lost with that intervention?*

*Perhaps the "holoflux blur"—that which occurs when we step out of objectivism and re-enter the embodied, flowing natural world—cannot be captured or explained. What if we find, both in the outside world and inside of me, that this movement is actually the most basic truth, the most basic fact? Perhaps every story or fixed form in art we come up with—to picture and picture-frame it—is a feeble attempt that is bound to fail. Perhaps the realization of this failure can be a driving force to be with and of the world, instead of being against and outside it.*

# Bohmian Art School Revolution

---

Hester Reeve

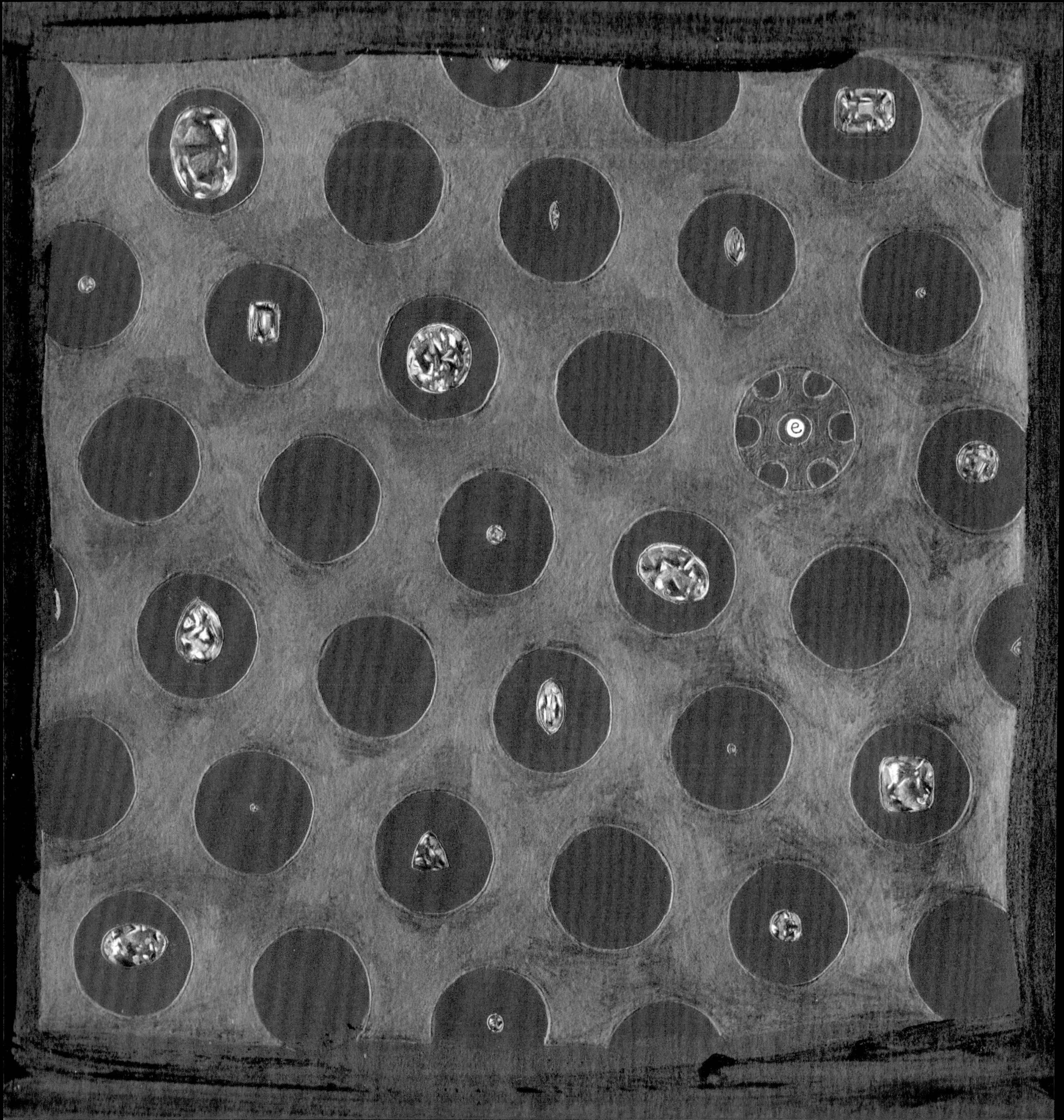

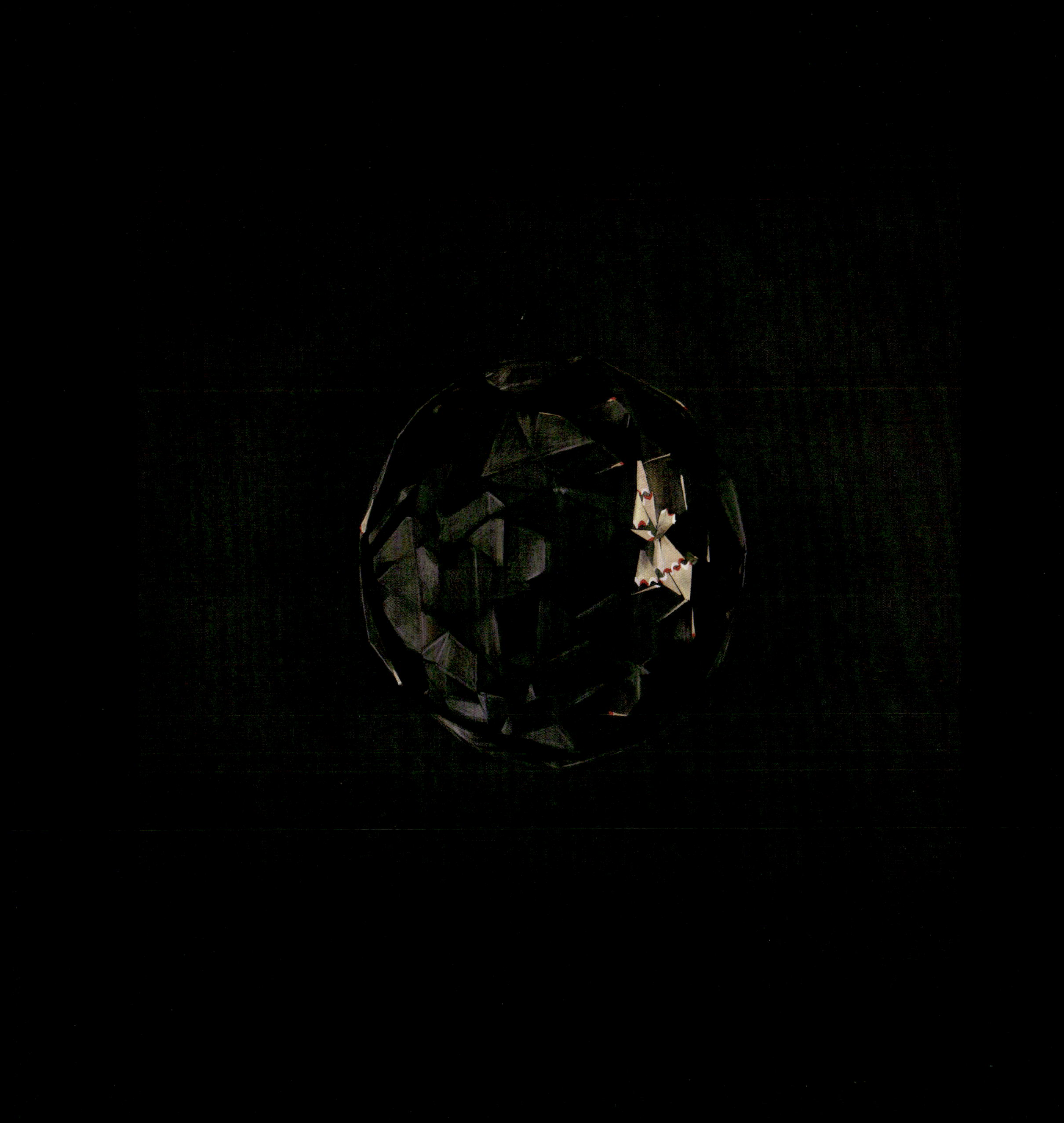

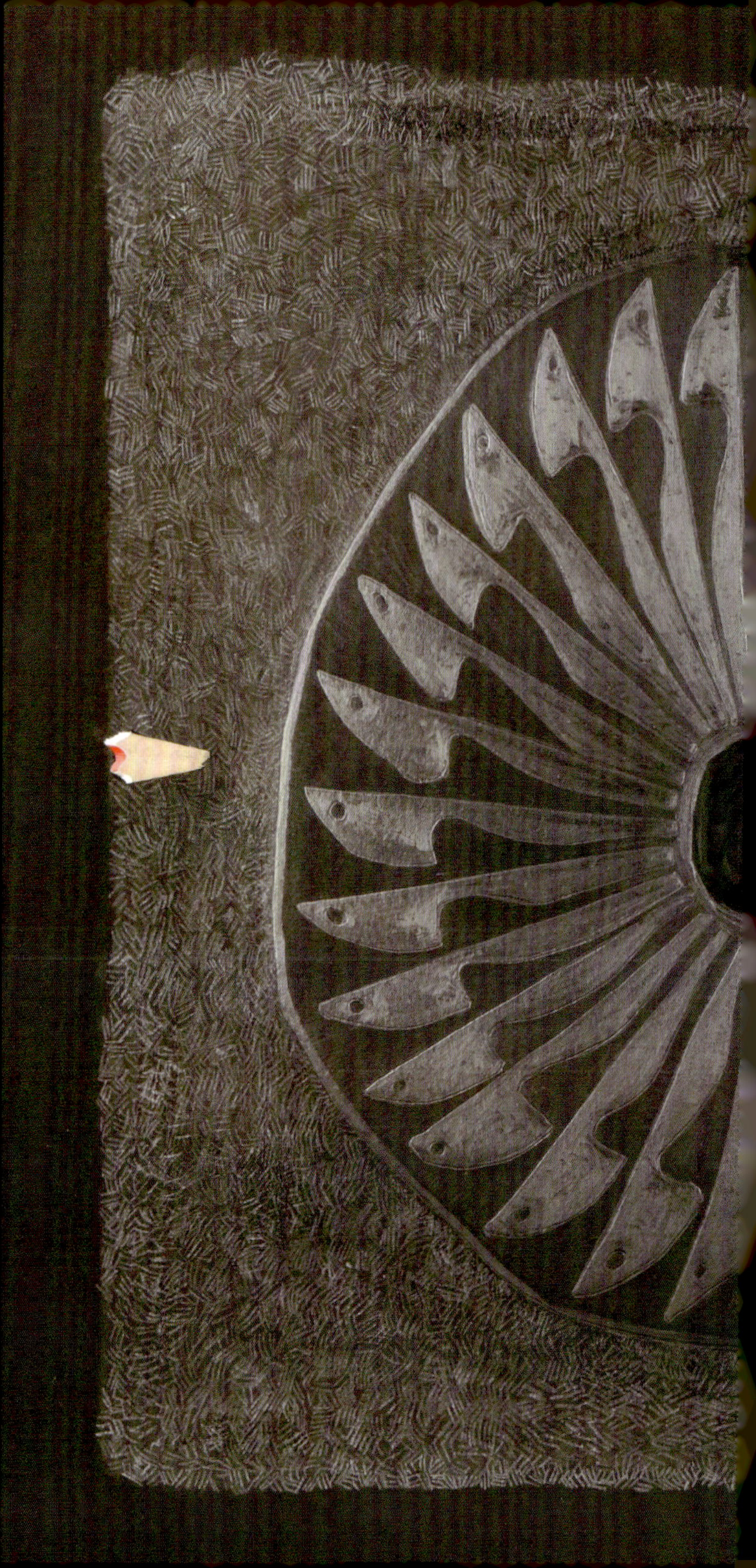

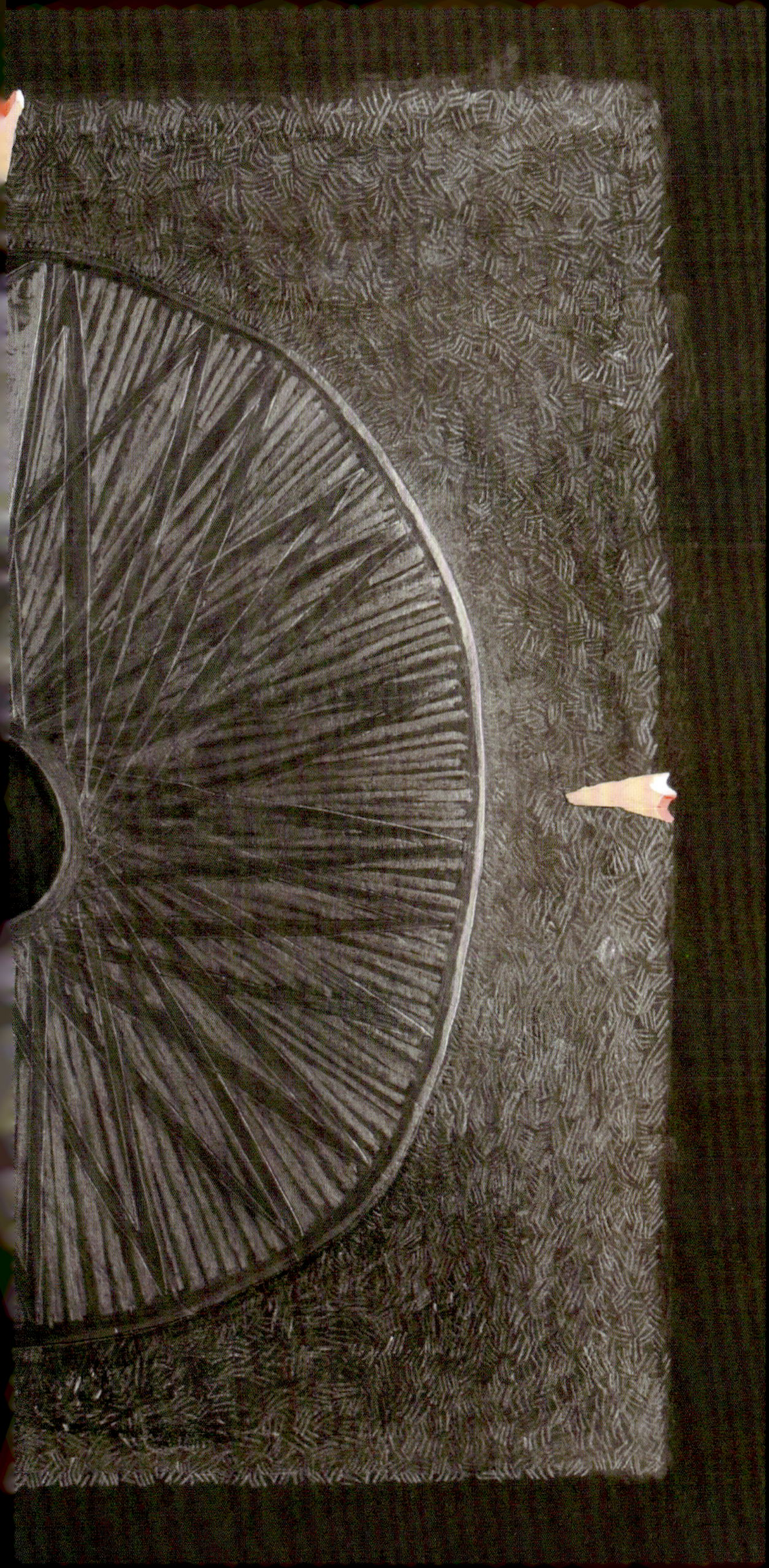

SACRED JELLY SPHERE : SPECIAL HERENESS

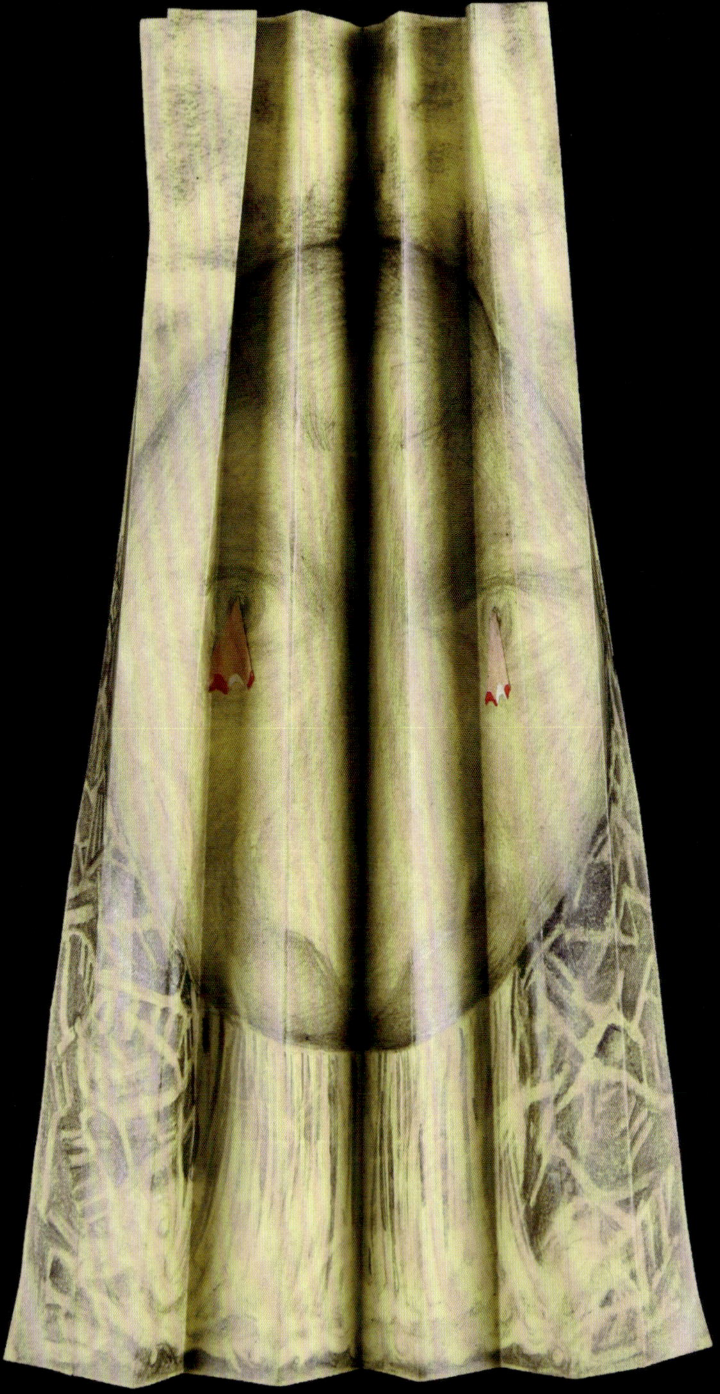

# HOWARD
## ART

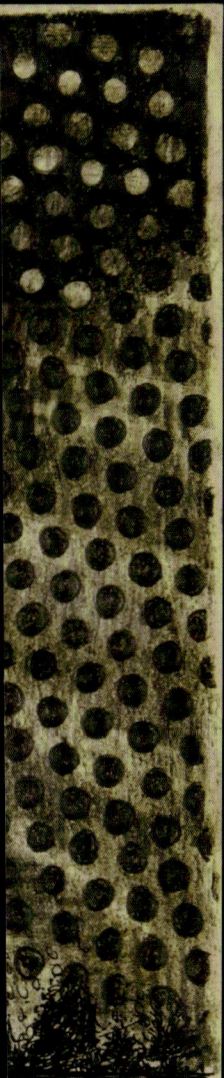

THE SUN DIRECTLY SEES SOMETHING OF ME HERE

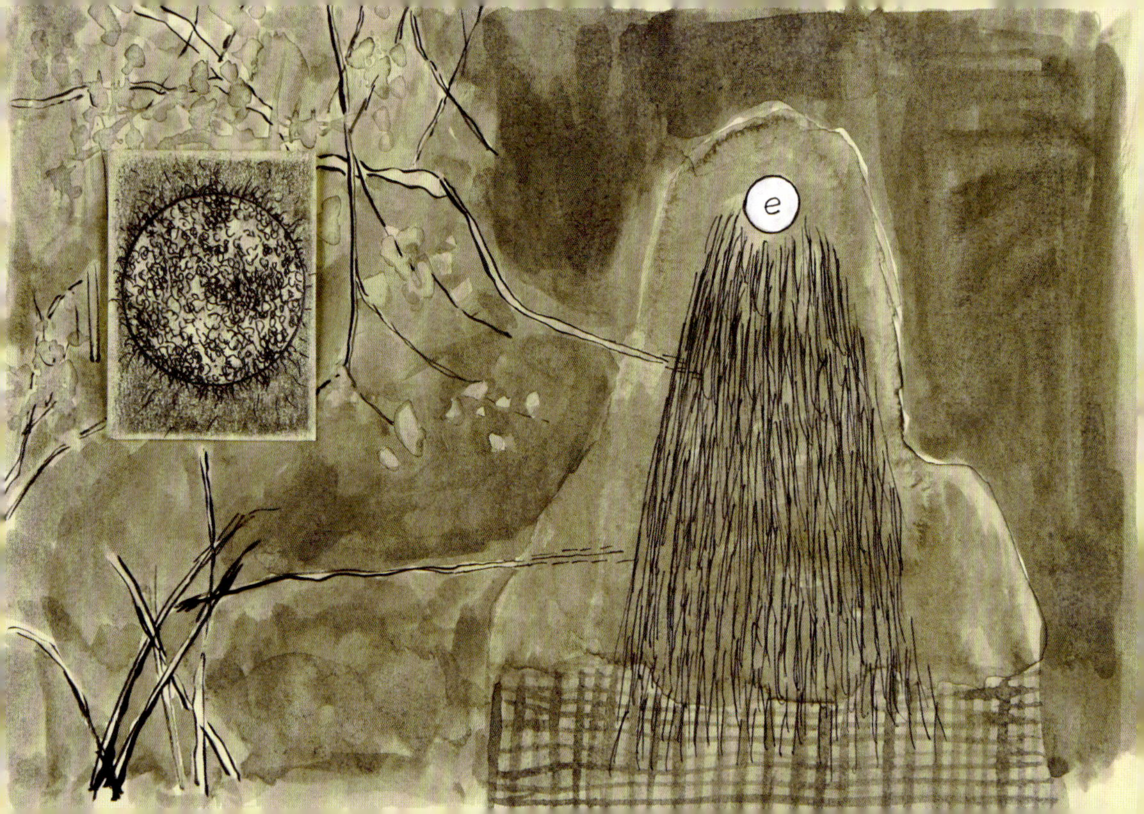
e

e

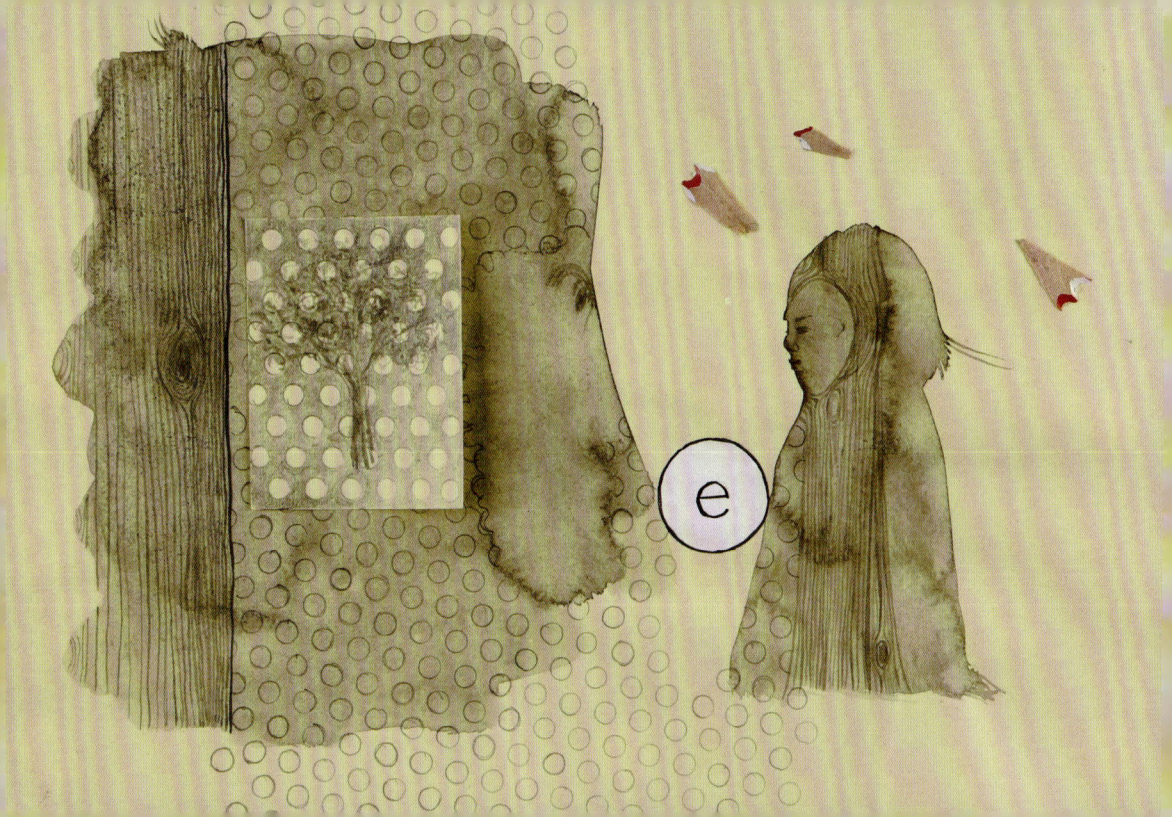

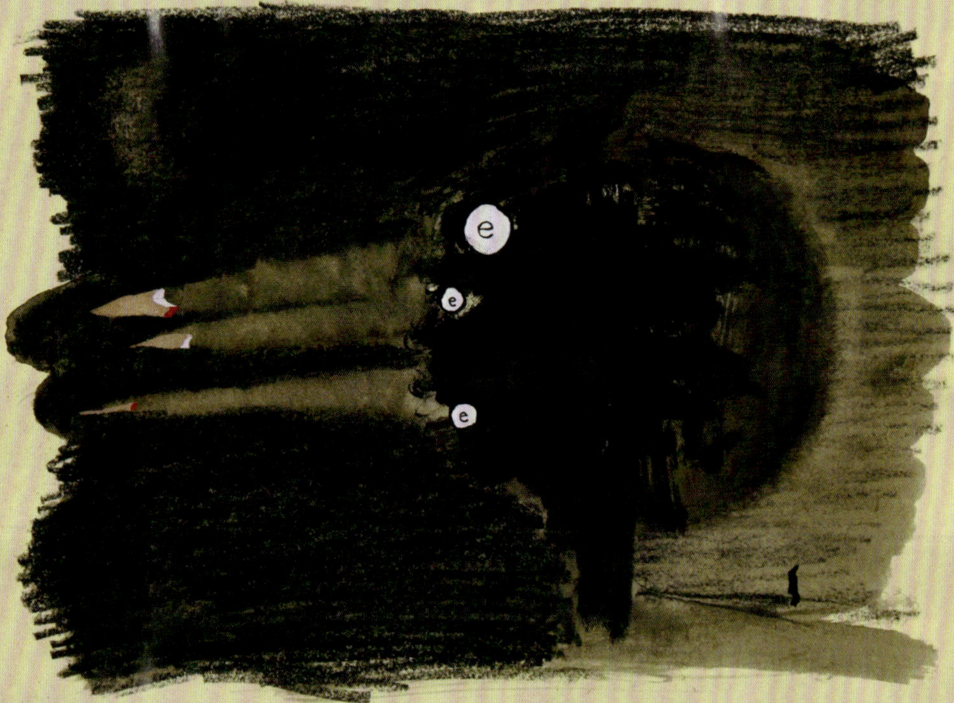
e
e
e

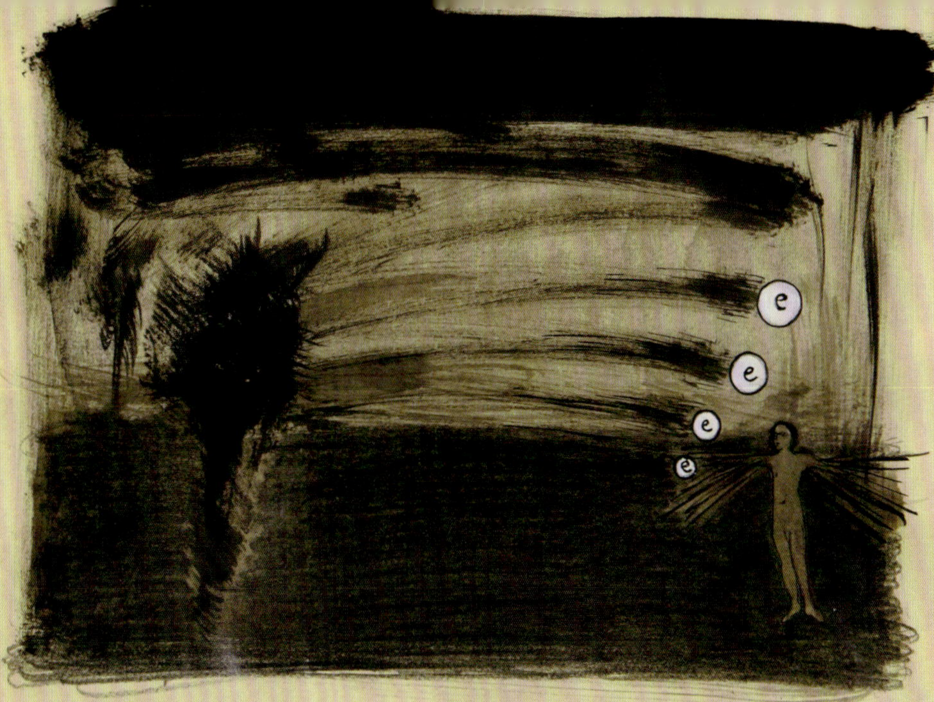
e
e
e
e

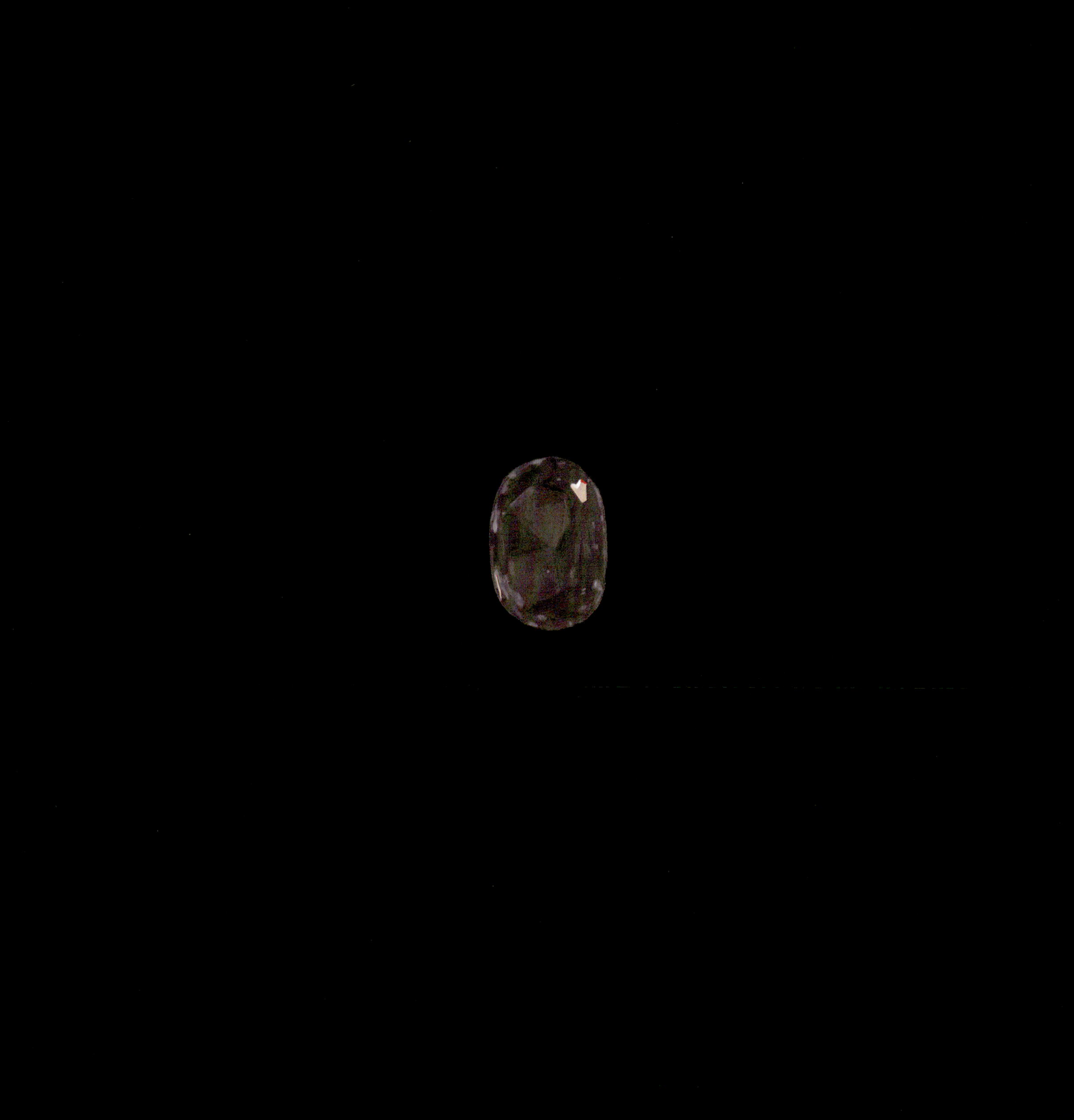

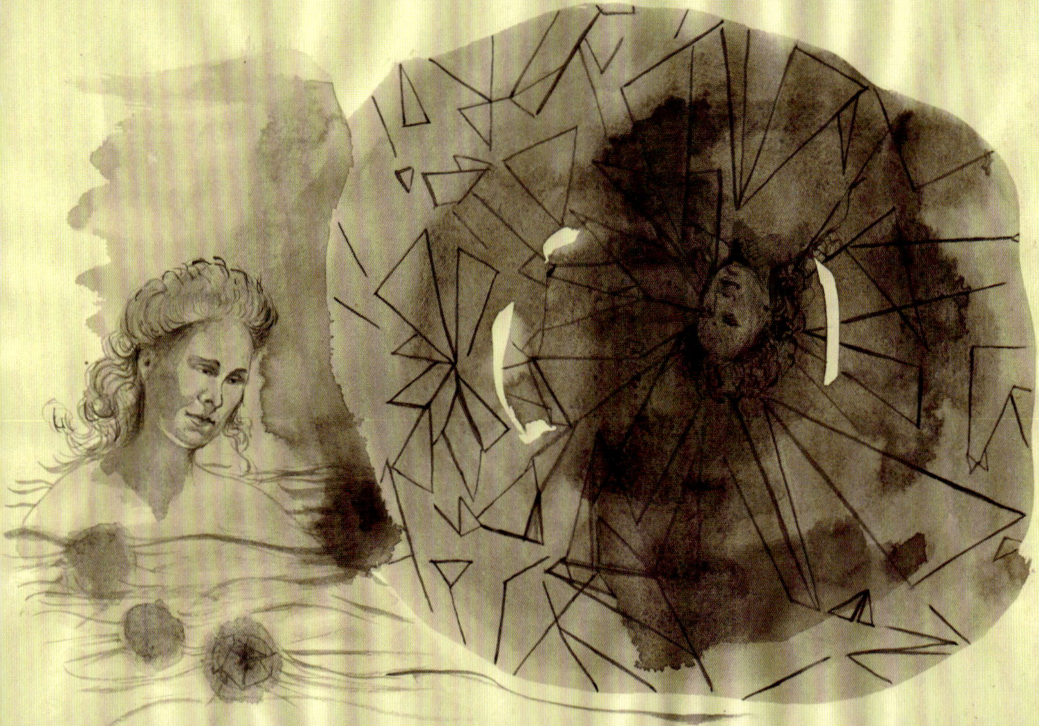

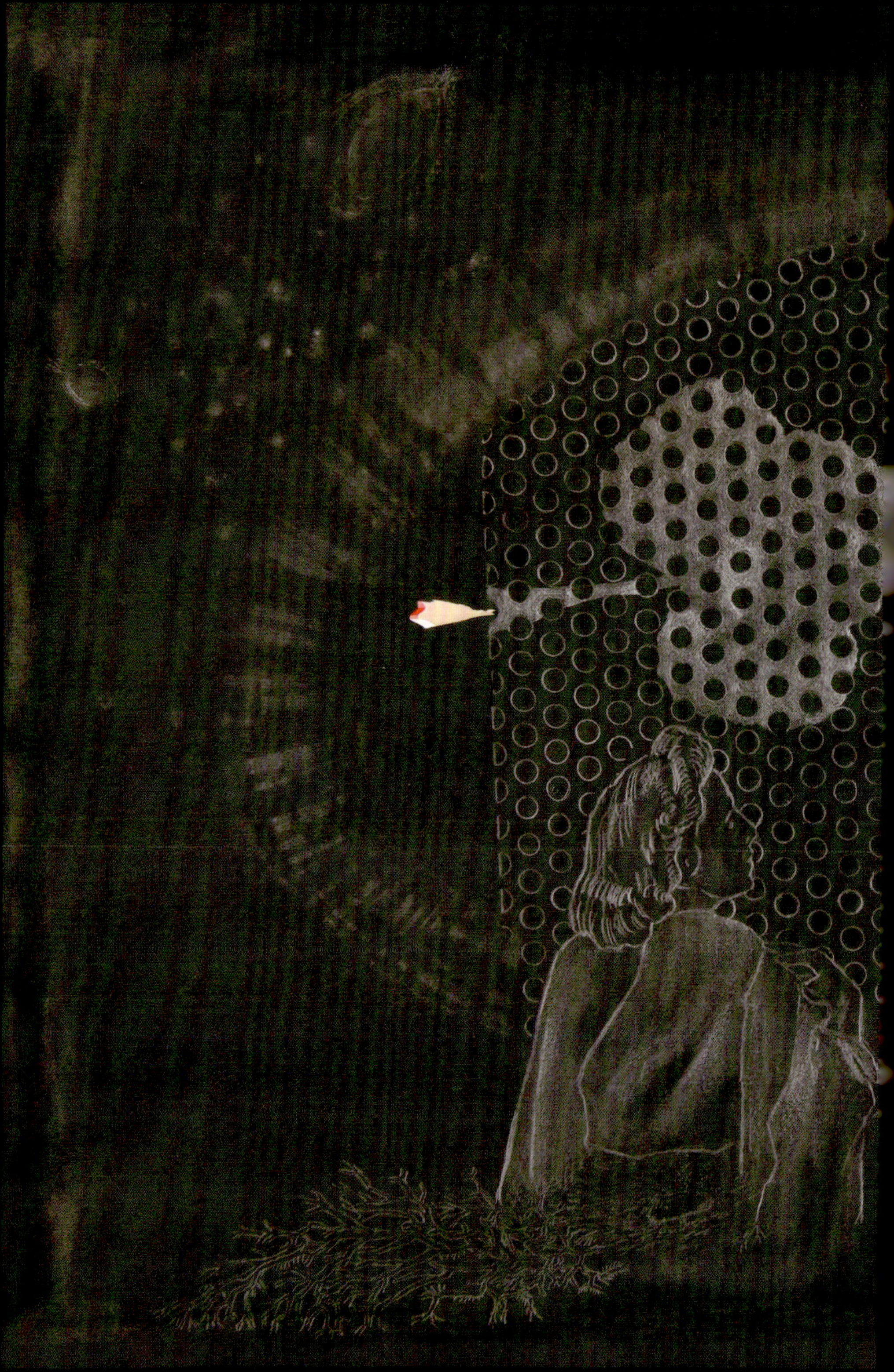

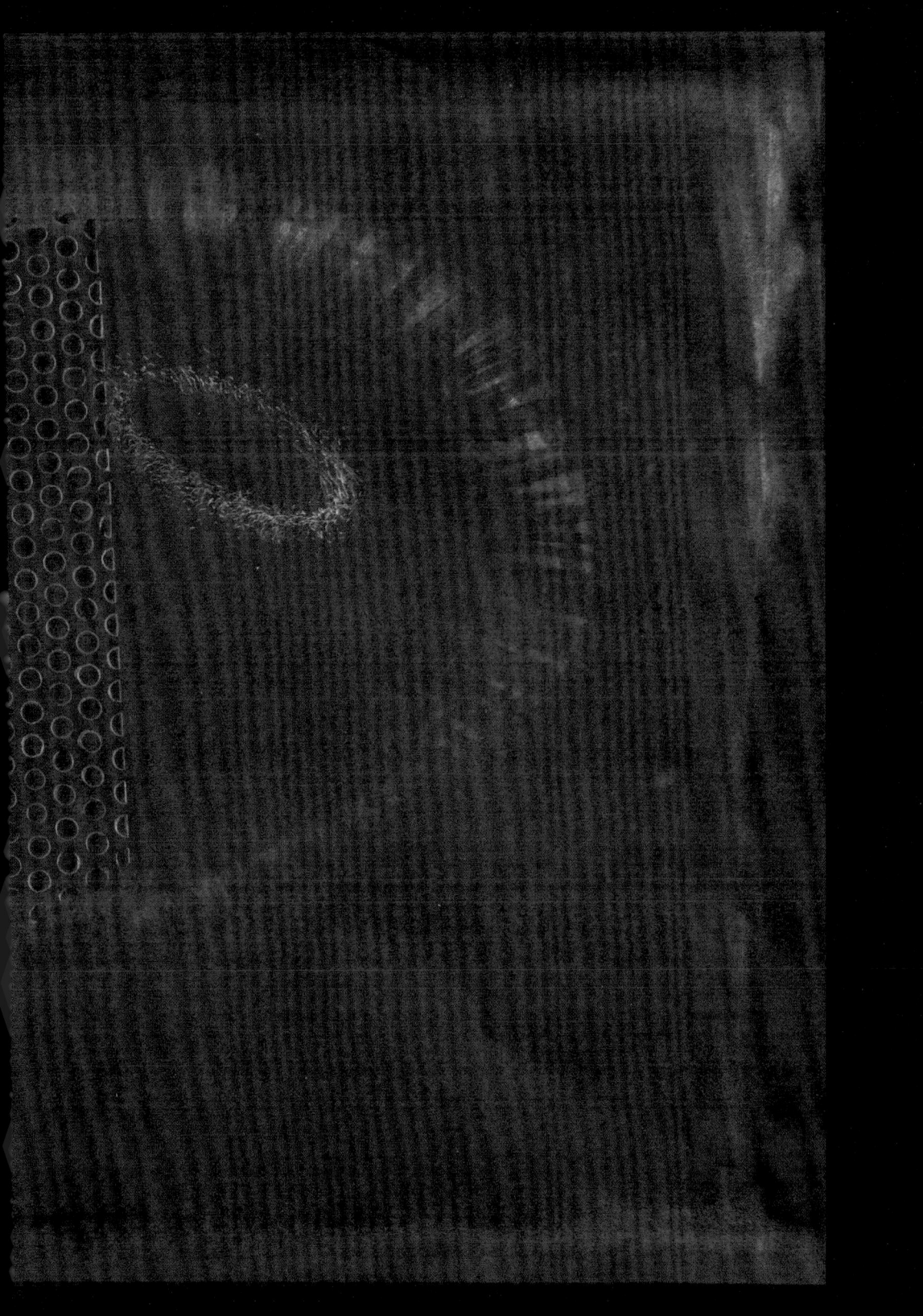

e

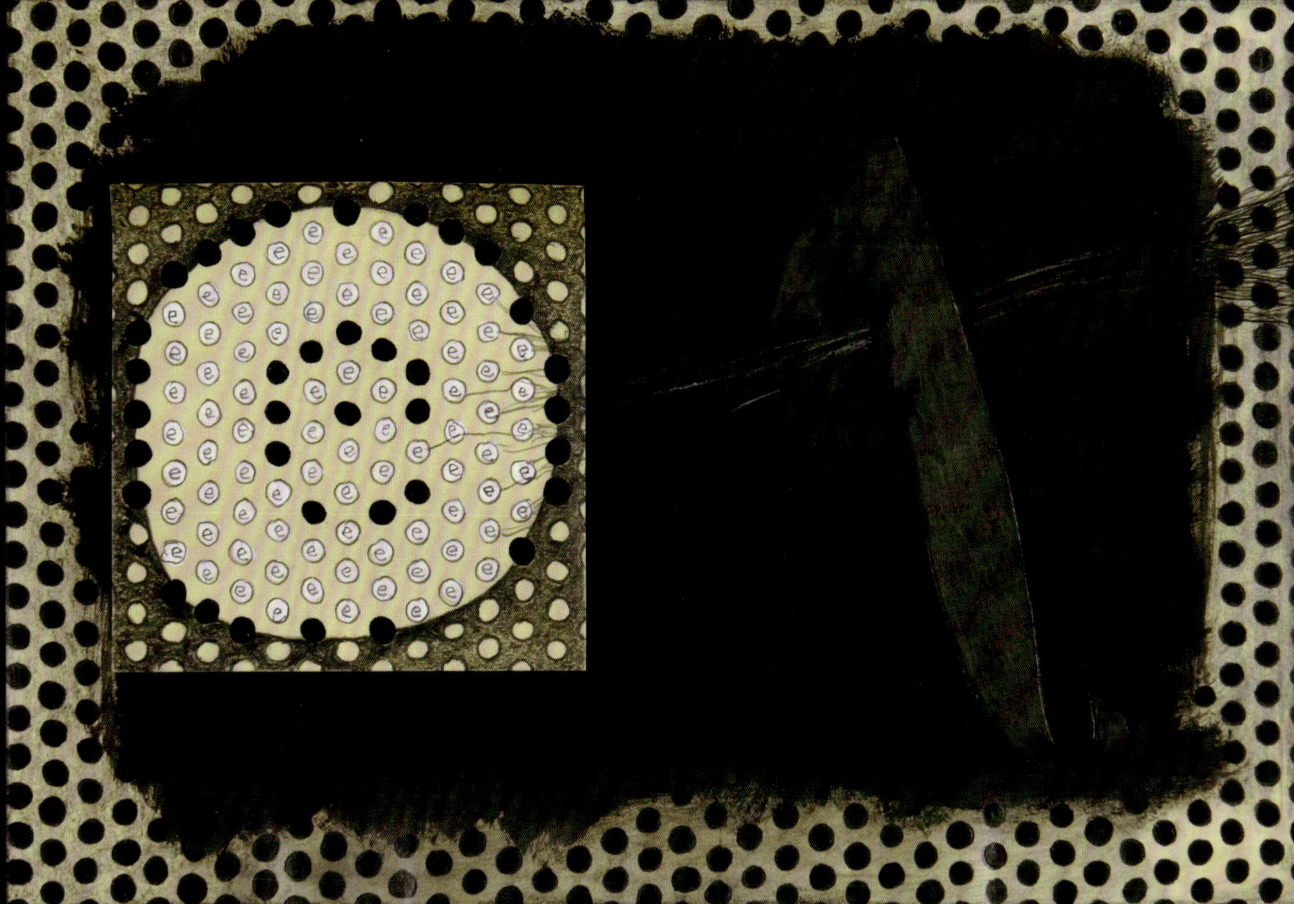

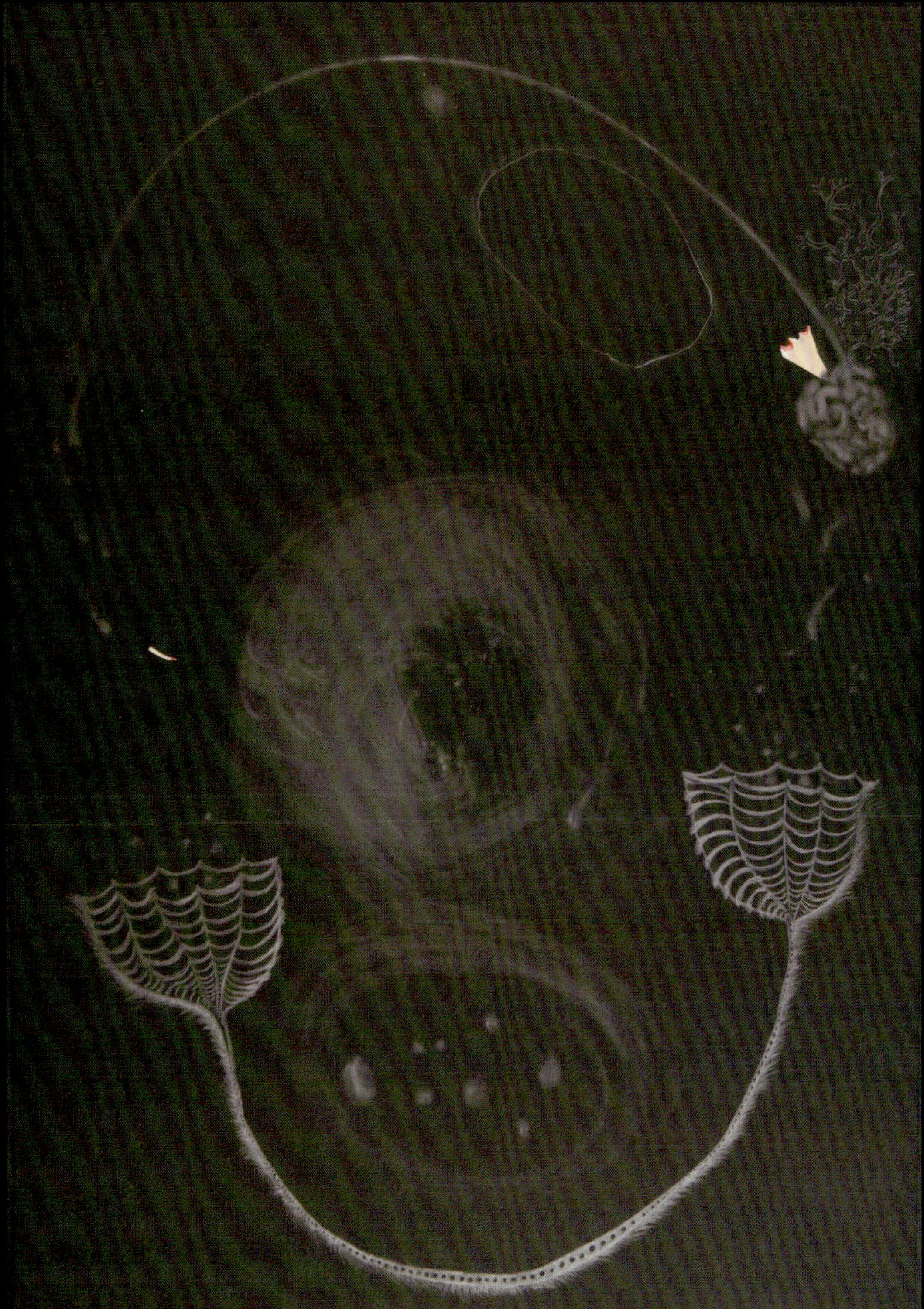

WORLD
WORLD
WOO

SUNLIGHT KNOWS AY HOLOFLUX LOCATION

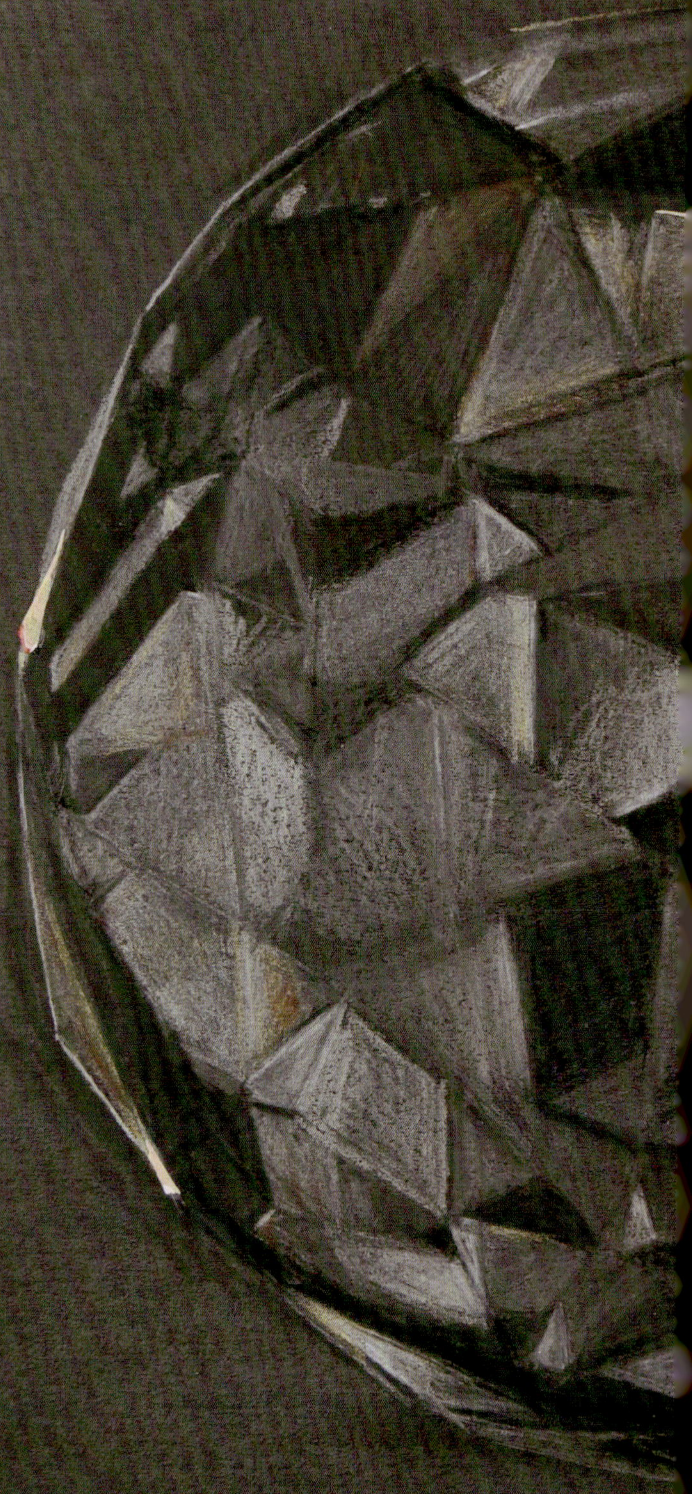

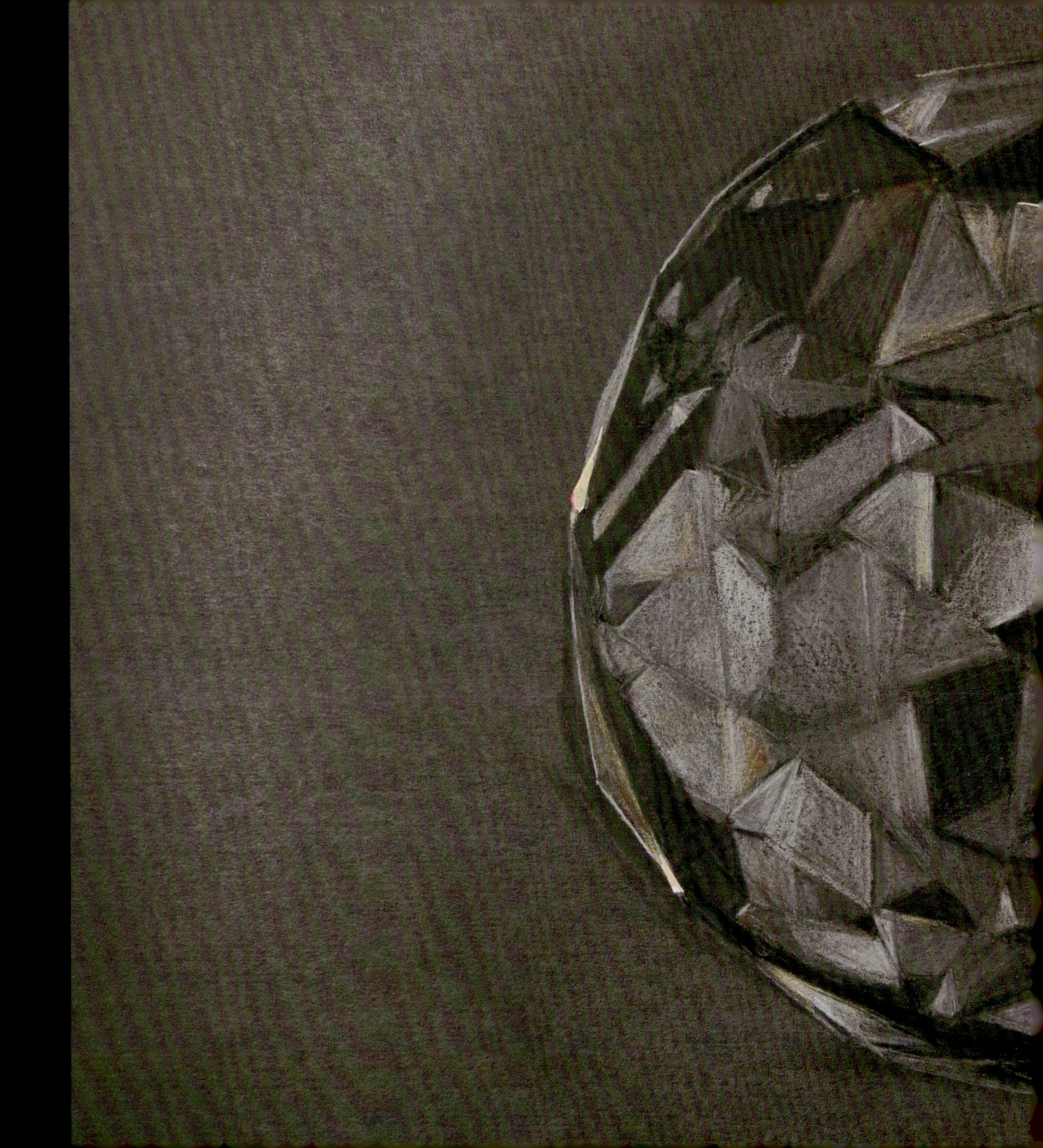

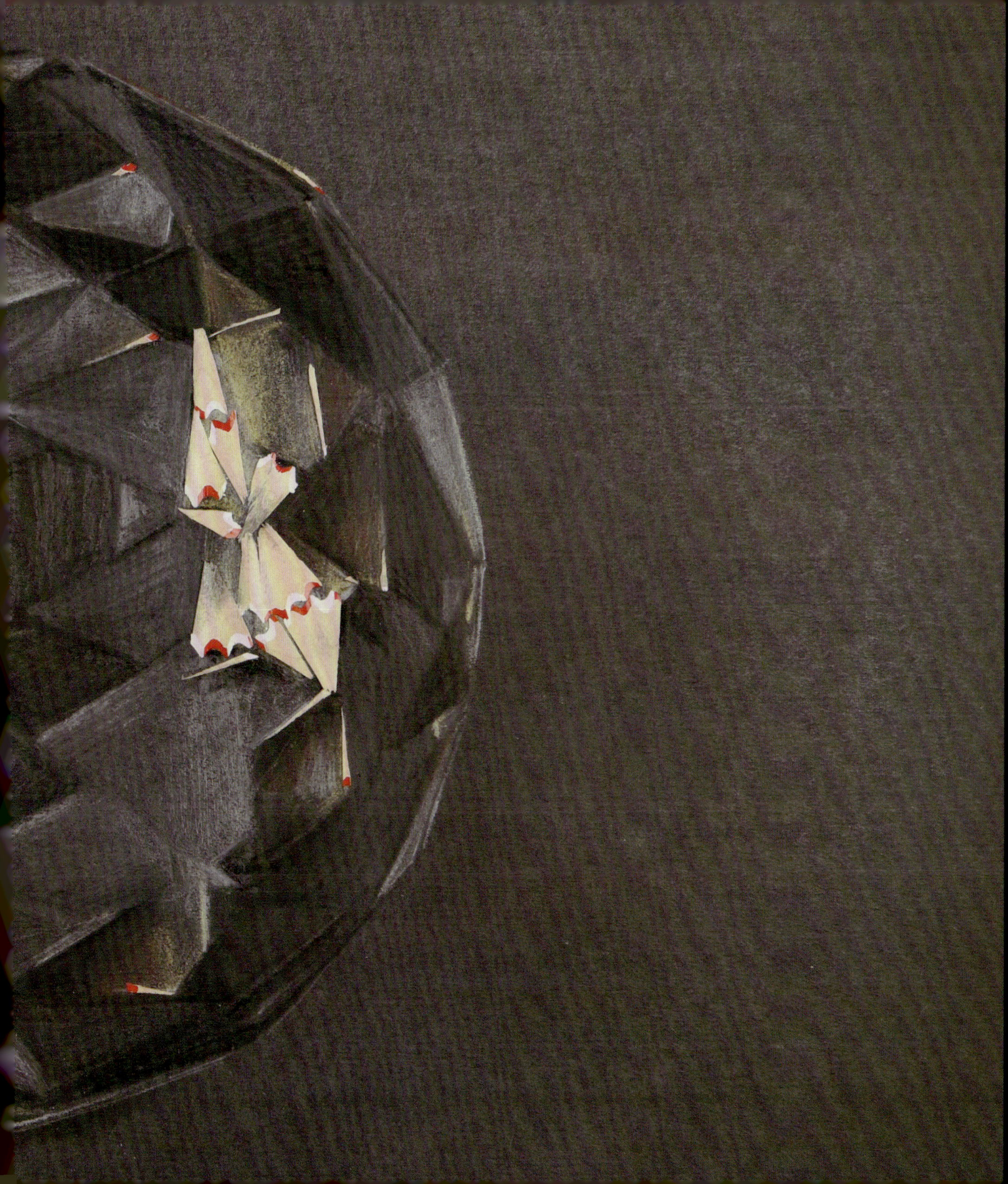

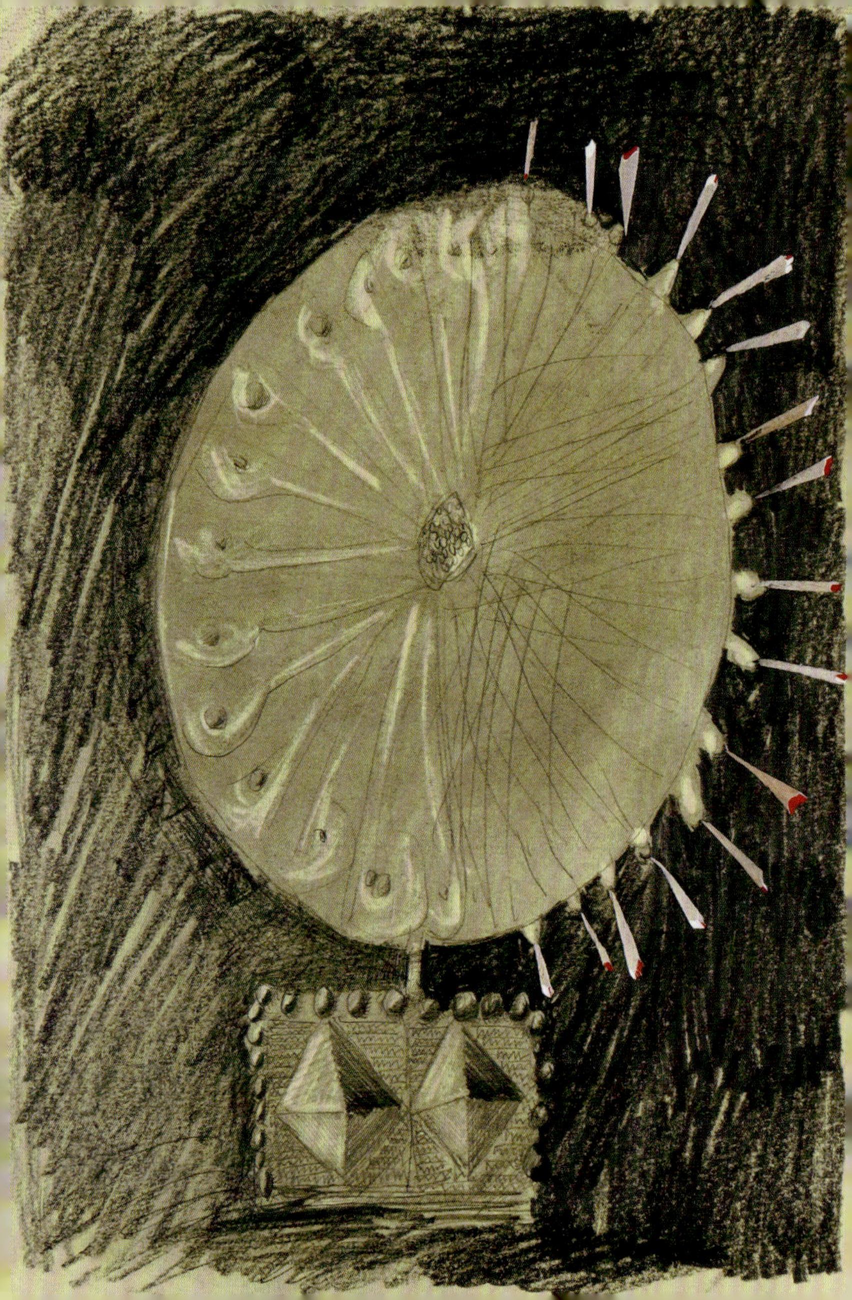

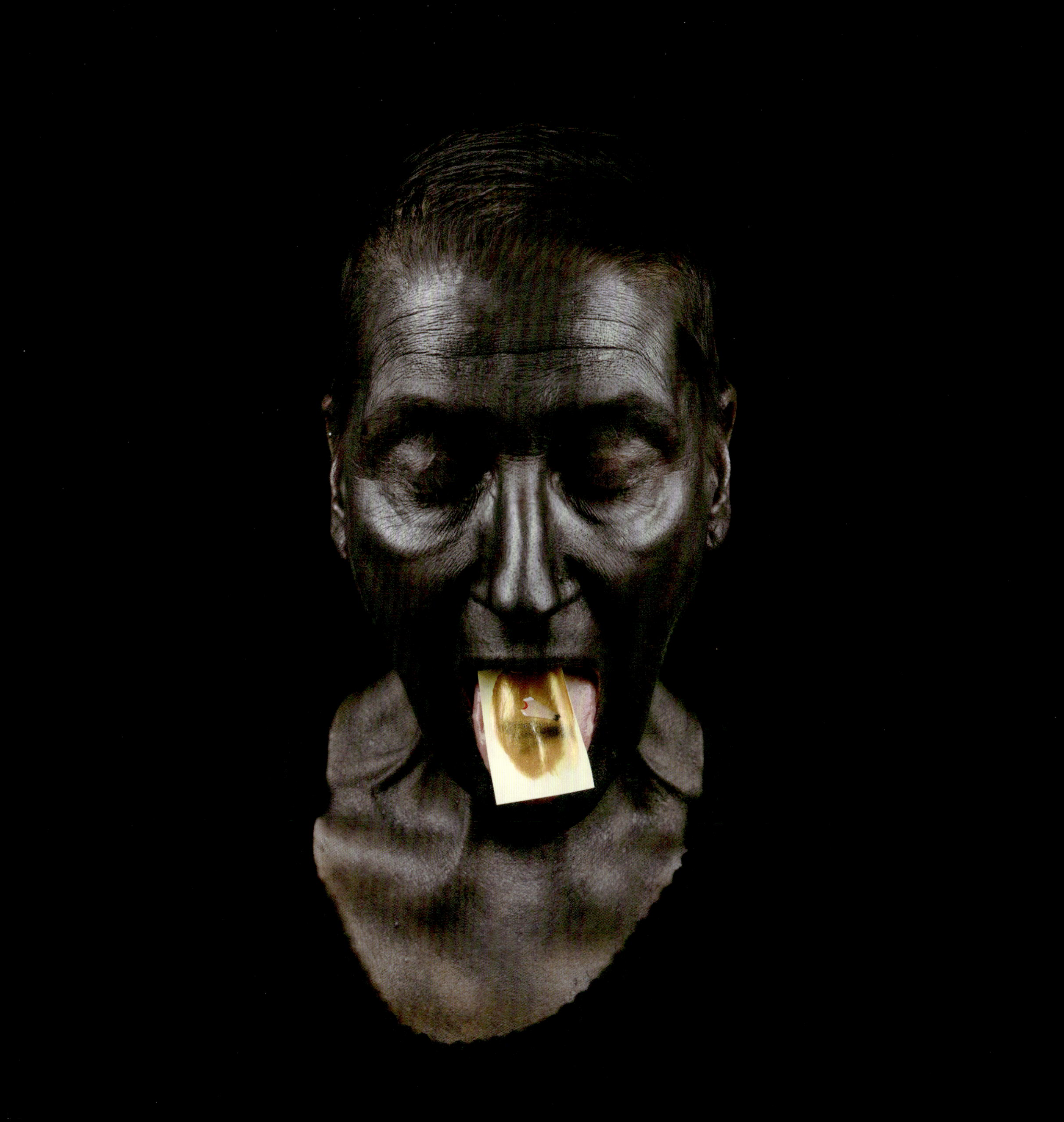

Sky 4

## *The infinite richness of nature…*

…as stressed by David Bohm, is the actuality within which human creativity can merge, flow, and intermingle. Previously neglected or unseen aspects of the world can generate new orders of artwork—visions that could trigger new connections, new sensitivities in the viewer, who will then look differently at nature when faced with a similar view as depicted by the artist. The same principle applies to any form of deeper questioning.

When we go to the heart of conventional realities, we need to challenge some of the fundamental assumptions. Our reflexive experience of the multi-dimensional world, for example—is it really real? Looking at a road or path disappearing toward the horizon we "see" the edges of the road converging in the distance. At the same time we know that most roads keep more or less the same width—and nothing whatsoever converges. In the end, what is real?

Another example is non-linear perspective. This way of "seeing" and depicting the world is considered passé, an artefact of less sophisticated eras, or the product of pre-adolescent consciousness. Our tacit assumption is that linear perspective is more developed, more real, more true. But to the contrary—non-linear perspective can provide a more realistic image of what it is like to actually be in or with the depicted subject, to be able to move around freely with the eyes, and perhaps generate space and time in different or more challenging ways, none of which are less authentic than the gaze of linear perspective.

Drawings made by young children, which are usually very much akin to ancient Egyptian perspective, tend to have a powerful somatic and lively character to them—so very real! Instead of forcing children to adapt to the "camera view"—conditioning them to assume that lenses and mirrors have a monopoly on objective reality and truth, we could break things open and allow multiple outlooks to nurture the imagination of the child. Adults generally have a great deal to learn—or rather unlearn—to become and remain creative throughout life.

Living more with questions than with ready-made answers can unlock the generative potential necessary to renew culture and re-think our current world. Because this attitude can be time-consuming and has no direct economic value, it rarely flourishes. Imagine looking at ourselves and the world from many different angles simultaneously, as well as feeling into it all, all at once, with all of our senses, generating a constantly changing kaleidoscope of impressions and expressions in consciousness, pushing our finite views and the importance of fixed memories to the background. What kind of self-world view would emerge?

119

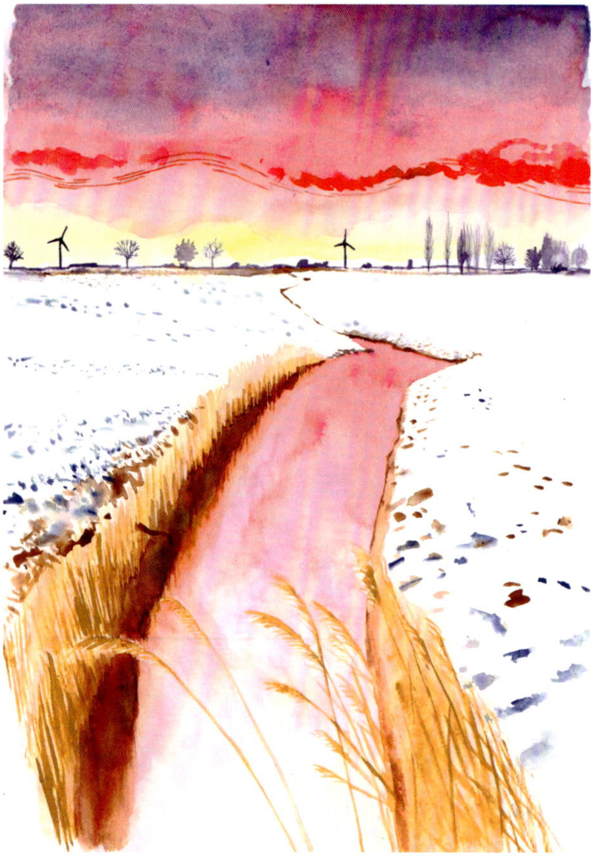

121

# Intermezzo

---

Beth Macy

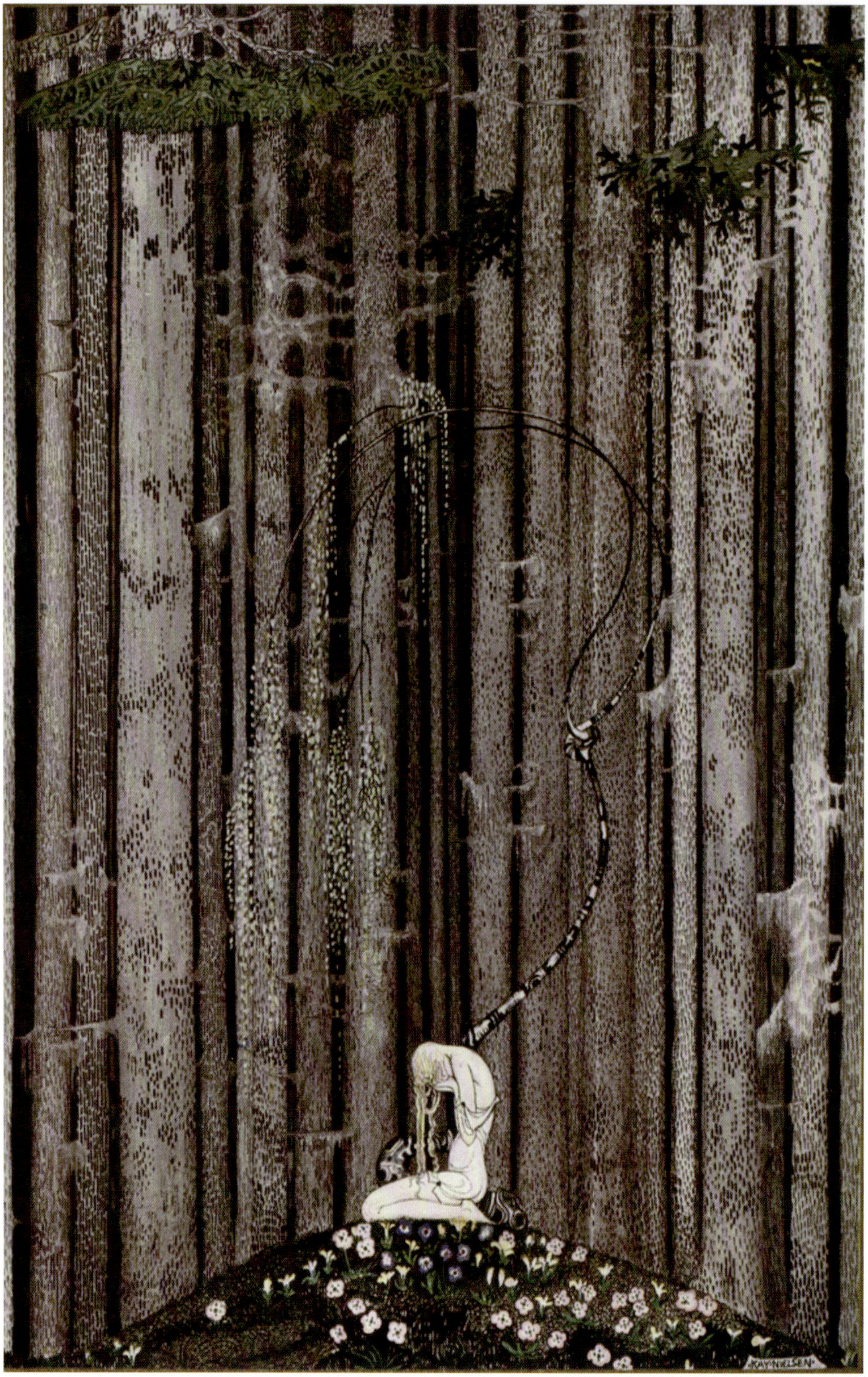
KAY NIELSEN

# Intermezzo

What is this?
….dream or real?….
….an in-between space….
….staying still and holding the spell….
….just being here….
….waiting, sensing, feeling, listening….
….what shows up to be noticed?….
….a scene or a song or a word?….
….whatever comes….

A voice
….oh, it's me!….
….crisp, quick, clear, telling, demanding, directing….
….and who is this voice of me talking to?….

Another voice
….oh, it's me, too!….
….soft, gentle, warm, melodical, comforting, enveloping….

Eavesdropping….what goes on between them?
….forcing ~ receiving….
….resisting ~ welcoming….
….holding on ~ switching places….
….joining ~ separating….

Oh, where is this headed?
….what's it leading to?….

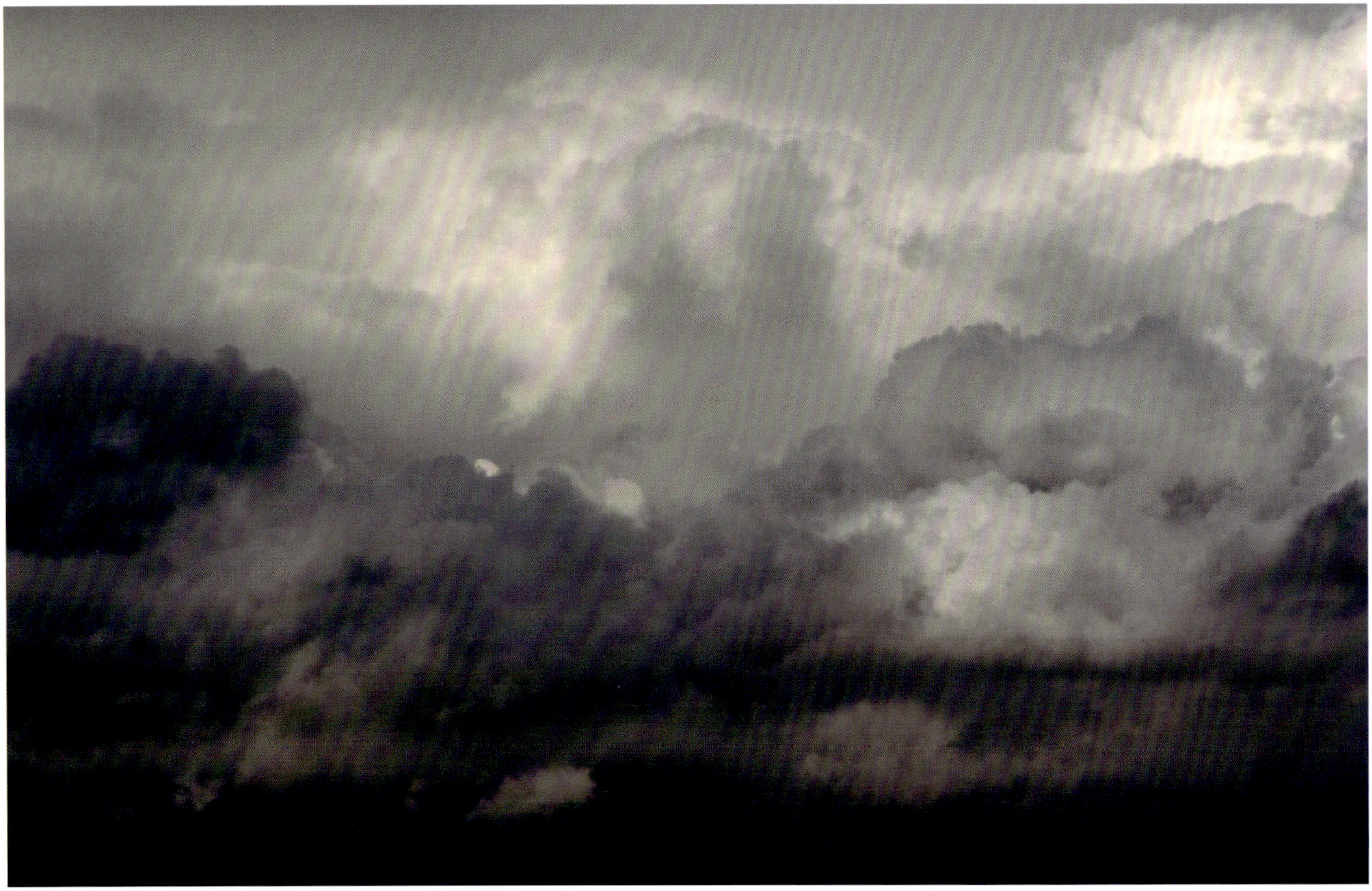

# Storming

**We need to talk!**

> Yes, but please not now. There's a big storm threatening, and it looks like it's about to hit. I need to pay attention to it.

**NOW!**

> OK, but please, just for a few moments.

**I was really angry when we last talked!**

> No missing that! Well, you weren't angry, you were enraged.

**For good reason! You had accused me....**

> Correction! I had commented on the impact of your thinking, or maybe the lack of it. And you didn't like what I had to say.

**Of course, I was enraged,
how else should I have been
when you compared yourself
to Job and me to the God
who had destroyed his world!**

*Yes, I said that. I still say that.*

**See, there you go again.
I had wanted to work this
through, to settle things with
you. But instead, you're just
retriggering me!**

*I hear you're upset, but the storm is
beginning, the rain is intense. Can
we talk later when it has subsided?*

**Next, you're going to accuse
me of causing the flood!
Do you think you're Noah?**

......did you hang up on me?

> No, I didn't hang up on you, but it's becoming more dangerous here. The thunder is intense, and the lightening is hitting very close. I could hear a tree or maybe trees nearby splitting as the lightening hit. And the wind is whining, no, it is roaring.

**I'm sure it's a bit scary, but you always exaggerate your fear.**

> I'm afraid, very afraid. It's so close.....

....are you there?

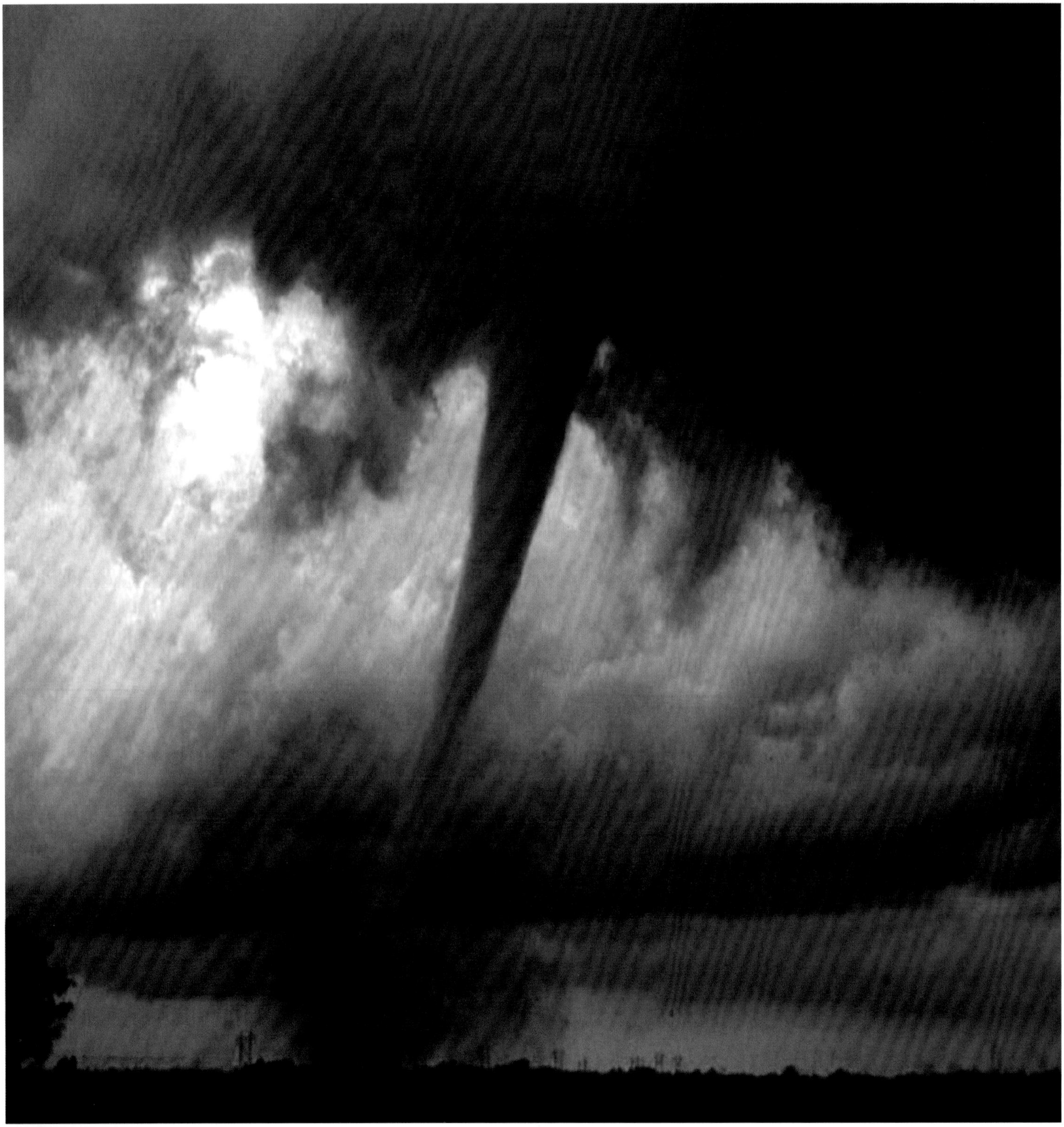

hello?.......

......are you there?
..........speak to me!!!!!

................speak to me!!!

...........................speak to me.......

.......................................oh, no! oh, no!

.....................................................oh no, something's wrong....

.................................................................Please, please speak to me........

*...the trees, Oh, My God,
...the trees...*

**.......Was that you whispering?**

*...the trees, Oh, My God,....
the trees....*

**The trees, the ones I planted in
the forest?**

*...ones you had planted...and
nourished....and loved...and
now....*

**What has happened to my trees?**

*…split, splintered, uprooted…*

**…oh…oh…but I so loved those trees…**

*…yeah. Me, too…*

*………………………………..*

*…are you still there?*

*….hello?*

*….what am I hearing?*

*….are you weeping?*

....I'm here....shall we talk?

What did you want to tell me about Job?

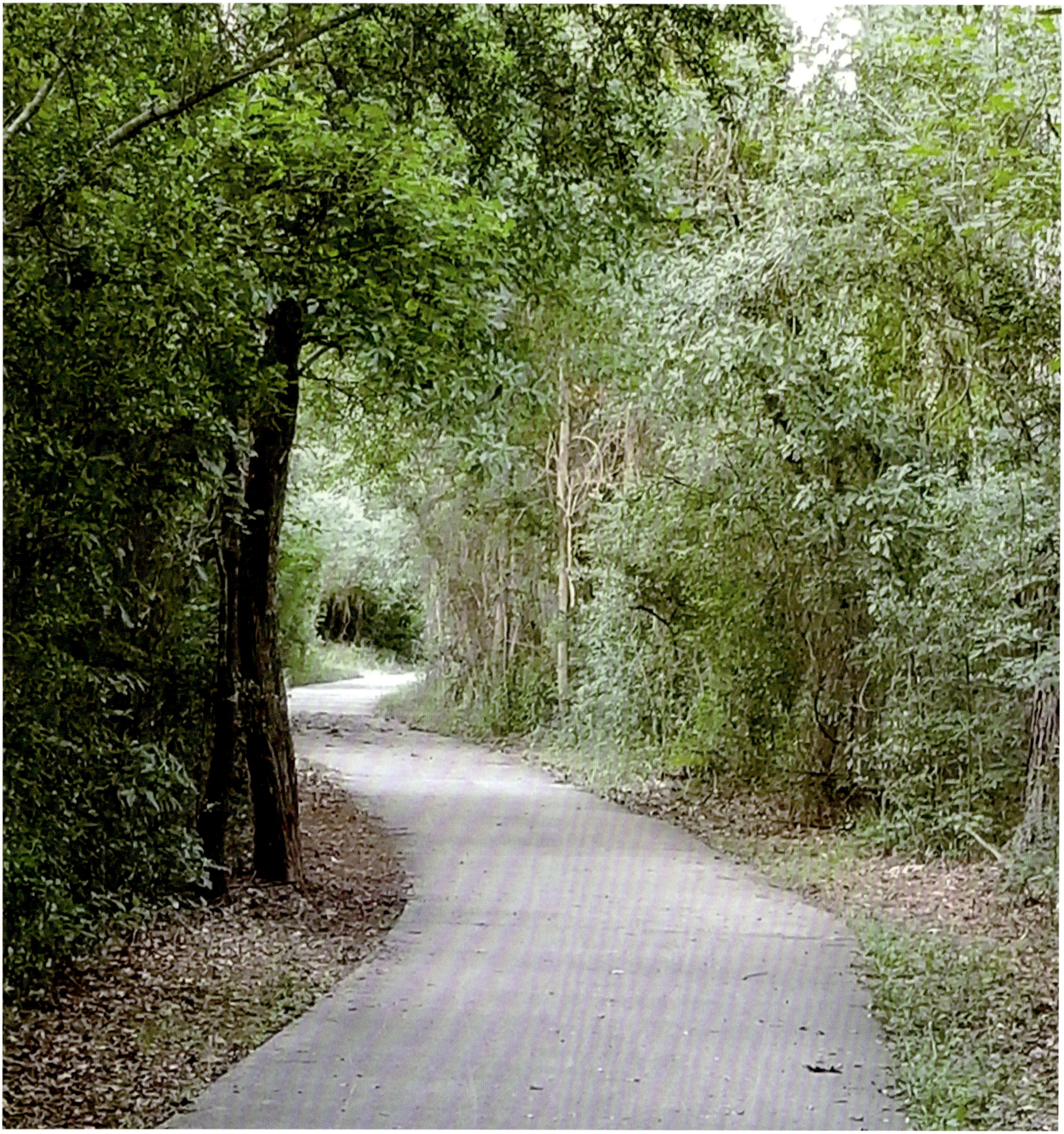

# Me and My Shadow

*How many times have we walked this pathway?*

**A hundred at least. I would have to check in my calendar to be sure.**

*No, no! I'm just saying I never get enough of it, you know, the idea of nature naturing!*

Look, there's my favorite tree!
Stop a minute, I want to look up
at it.

**What are you doing?**

Putting my hands on the trunk.

**Yeah, if anyone passes by us they'll
think you're nuts, and probably
me, too!**

Probably, so, but I love to feel the
pulsing through its bark. I can
feel my heartbeat syncing with it.

**Nice idea, I never felt anything
like that.**

Yet!......

**Right..............!**

**Uhhhh! Look at your shadow!**

*What about it?*

**Well, it's different than shadows usually are…look how transparent it is.**

*Yeah? ….what do you think that means?*

**I think your shadow is playing with you.**

*Yeah, right……….*

**Wow, look at the pathway!**

*What about it?*

**Pretty obvious, the dark and the light.**

*Yeah……and?*

**I've got to stop here for a moment. Can you feel this?**

*Feel what?*

**The air feels so balmy, like as if there is some thick perfume in the air…perfume with no scent.**

*Now you're really imagining things! It's quiet here, and there aren't other walkers here, but that's all there is to it.*

**It's so still….Oh, more than that! It's as if we just stepped into another zone.**

**Look, your shadow is pulling you....it's out in front of you pulling you forward.**

> *You are nuts! Come on, lets walk. I'm anxious to get back to the book I was reading.*

**What are you reading that's more interesting than this beautiful trail?**

> *It's very heady, you wouldn't appreciate it.*

**Really? I always thought heady books were the best. I'm surprised you're enjoying it.**

> *Tough reading, but the philosophical precision really excites me.*

**Oh,……………………………?**


**Oh,……………………………!**


**Ha, ha, ha! Do you get it?**

> *Apparently not what you're getting. Maybe it needs to soak for a while………..*

**Sigh………**

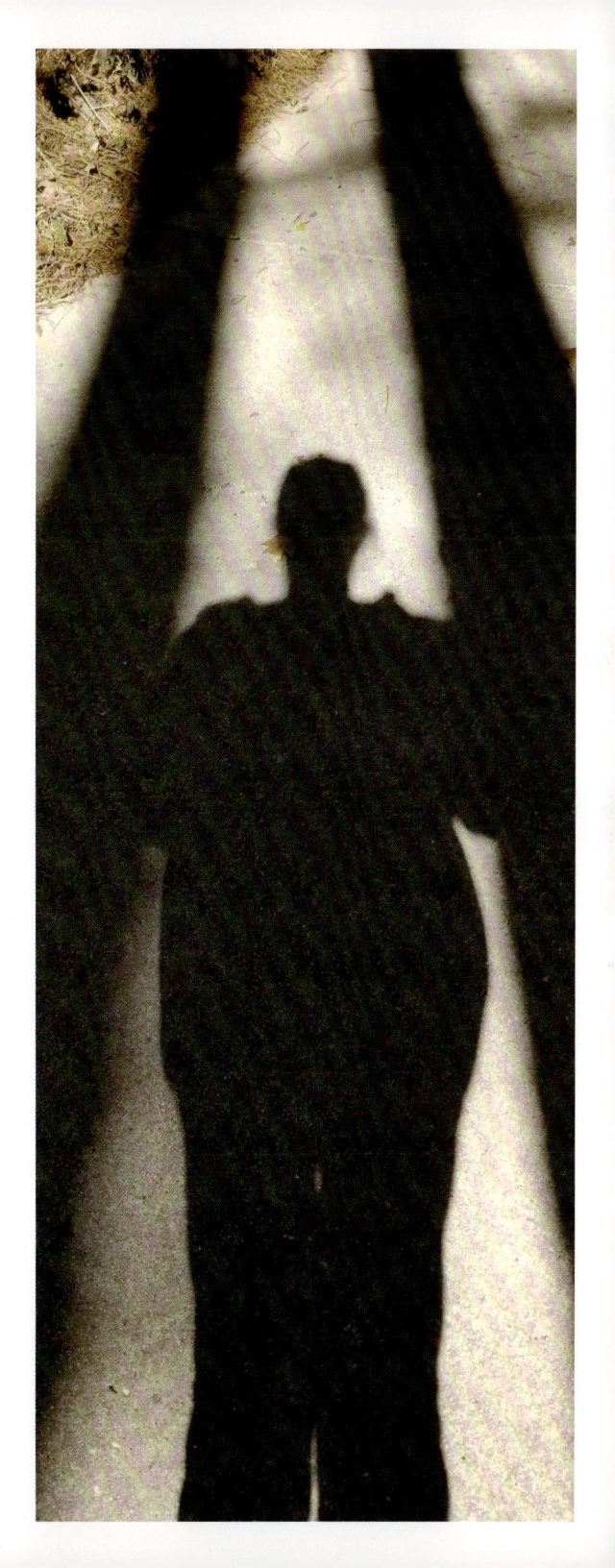

**You've been quiet for while. What's going on with you?**

> I was just off in my head pondering….remembering a few times in childhood when I got confused.

**Confused about what?**

> Well, about the boundaries between myself and others. Especially when very young, I used to wonder, "Whose thoughts am I thinking? Whose feelings are these?"

**What an interesting wondering! Do you still have confusions like that as a grown up?**

> Not so much, I don't have any idea why that sense came to me right now. Have you ever had that feeling….of being confused whose thoughts you're thinking?

**Uh, huh…….**

**………………I think you got it!**

> Were you whispering?

**Naw, just muttering to myself.**

143

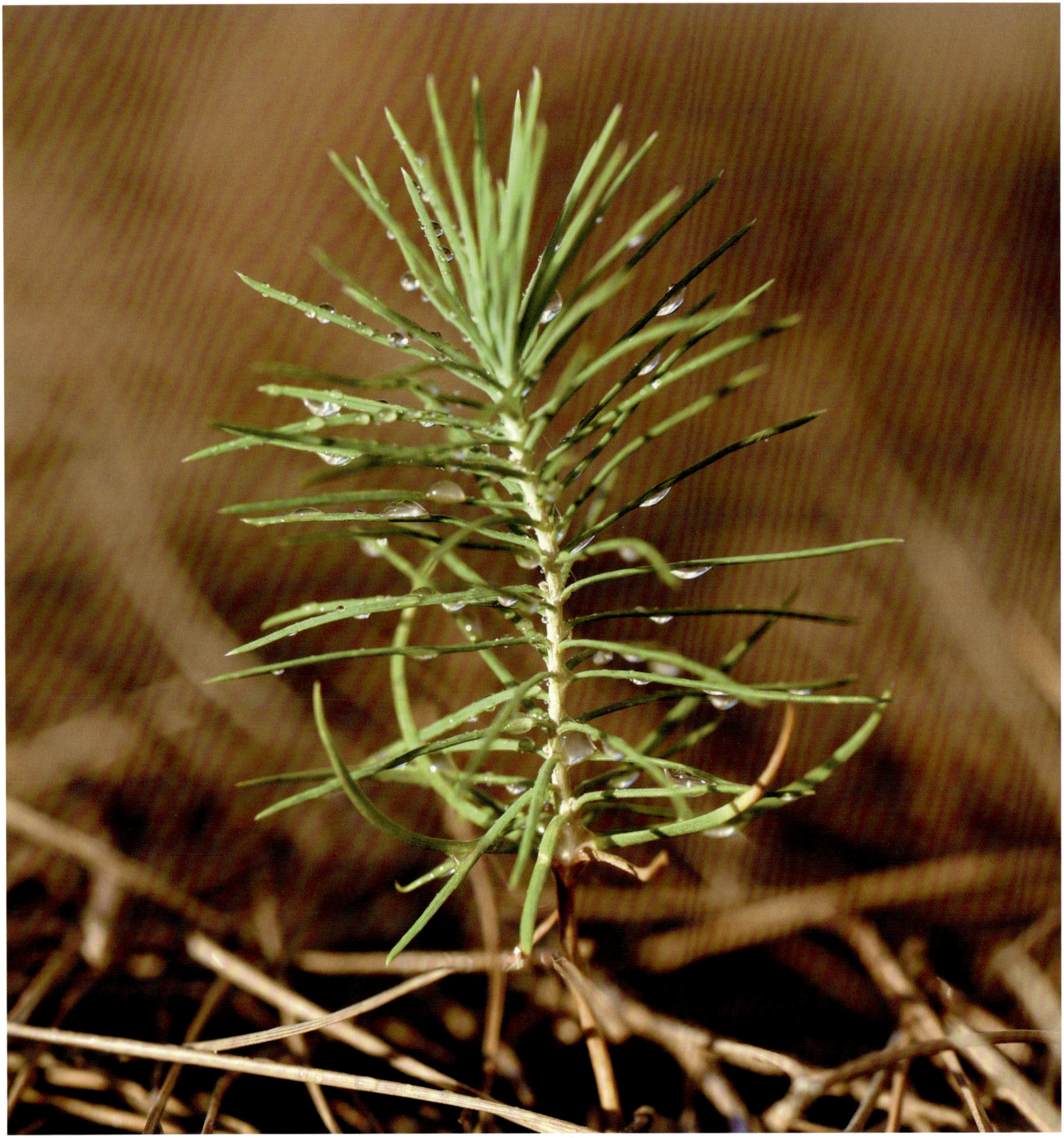

# Birth Day

*Today's my birthday!*

**Whadaya mean "*your* birthday?" Isn't it *mine* as well?**

*Oh, hmmmmm. No, I don't think you and I have the same birthday.*

**You think we were physically born at different times? Or, like born again?**

*No, no. One body, but I don't think you were there from the start. I don't remember you being there when I was really small…..it seems like you were born into the mental part of our joint mind-body later.*

**I never thought about this before.**

*Well, think about it now. Do you have memories of being really small?*

**Let me think for a moment……….**

**Help me out here. What are some of *your* real early memories, ones where both of us were there?**

*To start with, I just have snatches of you, phantom images, times when my memory seems like Swiss cheese. It's only lately that we seem to show up at the same time. That's new.*

**Yes, I agree with that, but try to go back to the holes in the Swiss cheese where you suspected something else was inside here besides yourself.**

*OK, hmmmmm, well maybe an early Swiss cheese experience was when I started kindergarten. My emotions were all stirred up....all the kids and a teacher I didn't know, and lots of rules....how to line up for the milk machine, how to color within the lines, how to know when it's my turn to talk. I can barely remember anything from that time other than my emotions, feeling anxious and scared, everything unfamiliar. Do you remember kindergarten?*

**No, I don't recall that.**

*That's pretty much how it went for quite a while…….*

*……Then there's a time when I was probably thirteen years old, after we had moved, and it had been hard to get settled in the new school. The Thanksgiving long holiday was coming up, and I dreaded being alone and lonely without new friends.*

**Oh, yeah, I kind of remember that. The history teacher had given an assignment to the class to write a short essay about Neanderthal people. I checked out several books from the school library, and during the long holiday, I was totally submerged in reading and doing the essay.**

*All that is hazy, but I do remember that my teacher was shocked to receive such a complete essay from someone my age.*

**I don't remember the emotional tone you describe, in fact, I wasn't aware of you being in the picture.**

*I guess I wasn't much there….maybe unknowingly I had passed the baton to you, and I checked out.*

**Let me get this straight, you were more emotional than you felt you could handle, and so to escape the discomfort you turned control over to me?**

*Not that I realized that was what I was doing, but, yes, as I look back now, I was overwhelmed, feeling emotional about the situation I was in. I didn't recognize you were there, I just checked out.*

**Perhaps then, that was my birthday....when you checked out and I had gained enough ground that I could step in.**

> *Yes, good thing you did. But, you know, you've been a tyrant almost ever since then!*

**Well! One of us had to run the show! You've just admitted you weren't able to do so.**

> *True, but you can be so cold, so sterile, so logical and unfeeling while you're running the show.*

**I get quite weary of your moodiness....you can be quite irrational, you know.**

> *Well! Someone has to handle the feeling stuff, and it seems to be me....that has become my sole burden! Don't you ever feel you have some responsibility there?*

**Of course, but I don't seem to make such a big emotional fuss about it that you do. I just wait for the flash of insight, you know, the logical meaning of whatever it is, to come to mind.**

> *You think you're the only one who perceives meaning? Geez, no wonder we get in these conversations!*

**……………………………………?!**

> *………………………… ……..!?*

*………So……let me see if I can put this conversation together. On one hand there's your dominance, your accomplishments, logic, sterile coldness. And on the other hand, there's my emotionality, my empathy, my feeling things through. Is there no bridge between? How do we make meaning of this?*

………………………………………

*….I mean, why does one human have two such divergent parts? I don't get it.*

……………………………………

**…….I dunno. Best to let your question settle in some…….**

151

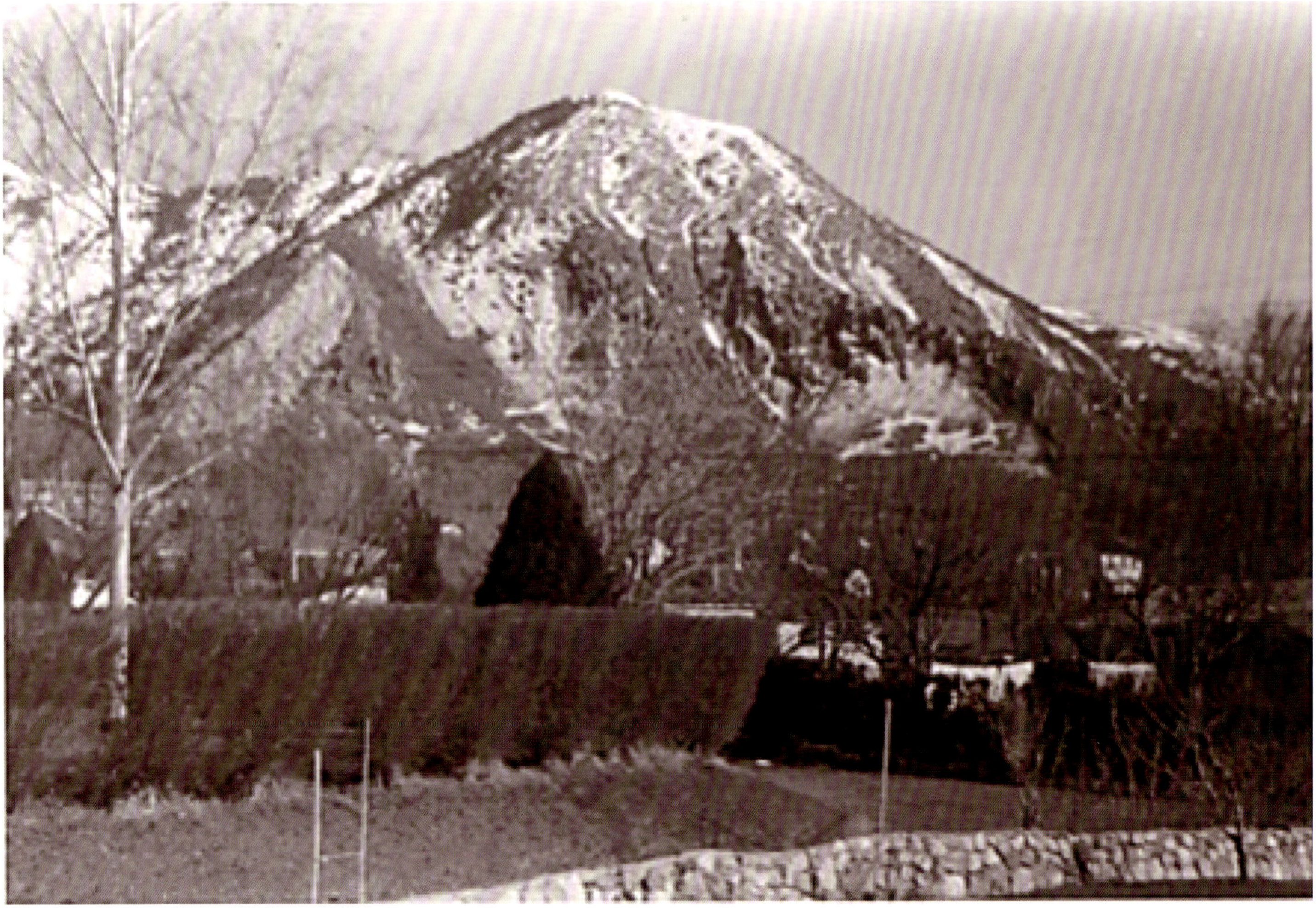

# Mountain

You know, I've been thinking that whole period of time after we moved should be called "Neanderthal!"

**How's that? Did you keep working on that essay?**

No, no! I'm not an essay writer, that must be your job! No, what I'm thinking is that period of time was prehistory in my life! I'm thinking that the patterns for much of my life that came afterwards formed then.

**Well, if it set your pattern then….hmmmm. Did it set mine as well? What's making you think it was so important?**

It's this memory that keeps popping into my mind. It was a few months after that first one we talked about before. I was feeling even more isolated and alone.

**No place you felt you fit?**

Ummmm, kind of. I did feel that I fit in with the beauty of the area, you know, there was our house right at the base of those beautiful red mountains.

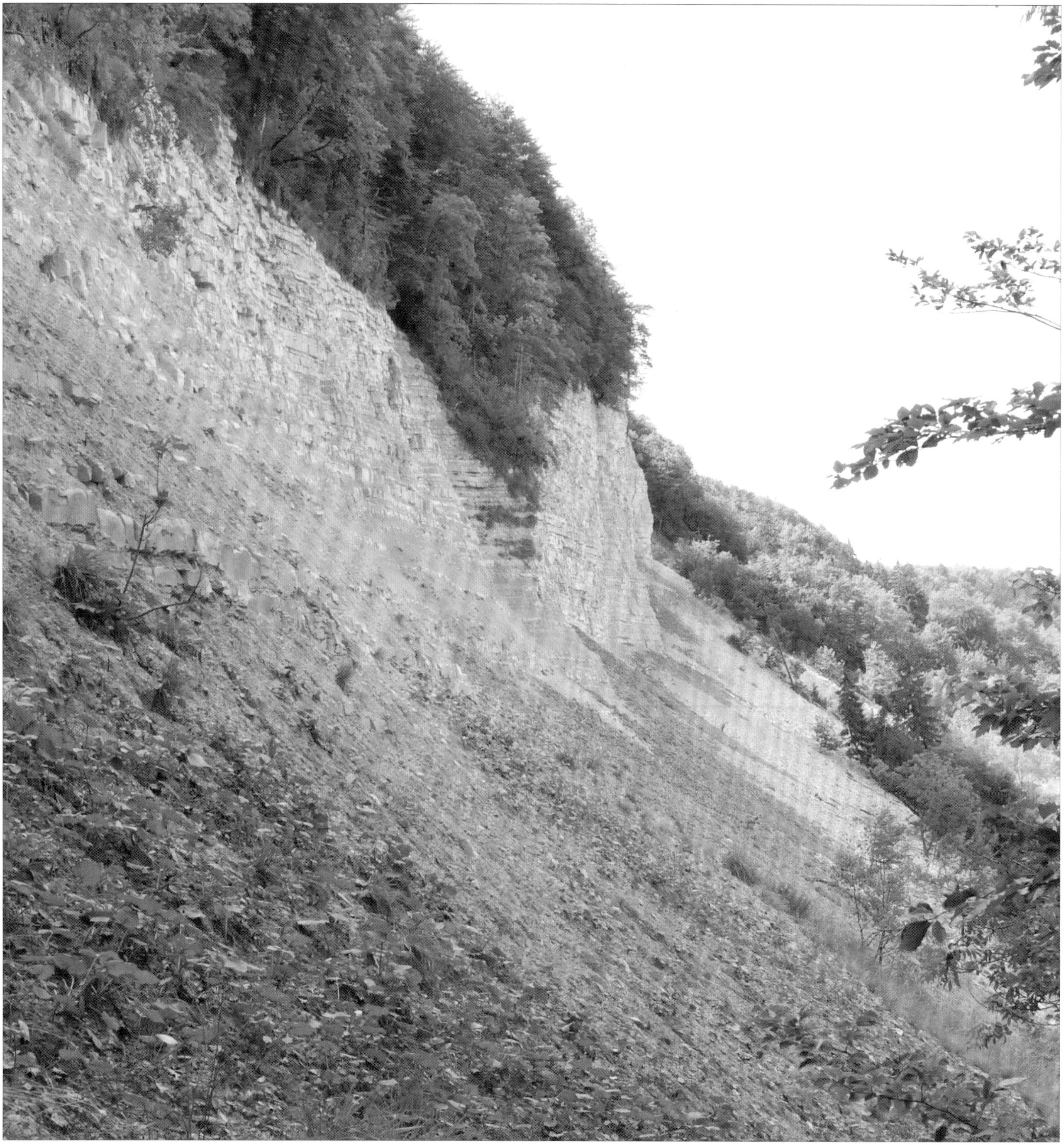

**Yeah, I remember that, too. I used to walk up to the end of the street and pick up the chunks of stone that had fallen off the craggy face of the peak and landed right there at the base.**

*I think I still have some of those chunks with all the mica that sparkled so! And that peak that I could see from the back yard, it was special. That pinkish-red granite on its face. Having such a huge piece of nature right there almost in my backyard, well, that was something else!*

**A great memory. Is that part of what made such a strong pattern in your mind.... well, in your part of our mind?**

It's about that....an experience I had with the mountain.

**Tell me, I'm anxious to see if I remember it, too!**

Ok, well, I woke up one night. It must have been two or three o'clock. I had a sudden urge, really a compelling sense, that I should go out to the back yard. It had something to do with that mountain. And then, I was suddenly cranking open my bedroom window and taking out the screen.

**Oh, this is exciting! Then what?**

Well, I climbed out and began walking in the grass. Oooo, I can still remember the feel of the dewey grass under my feet. The moon was really bright and full with those wispy clouds. And then I glanced in the other direction at the mountain…………………..

**Don't stop! Keep going.**

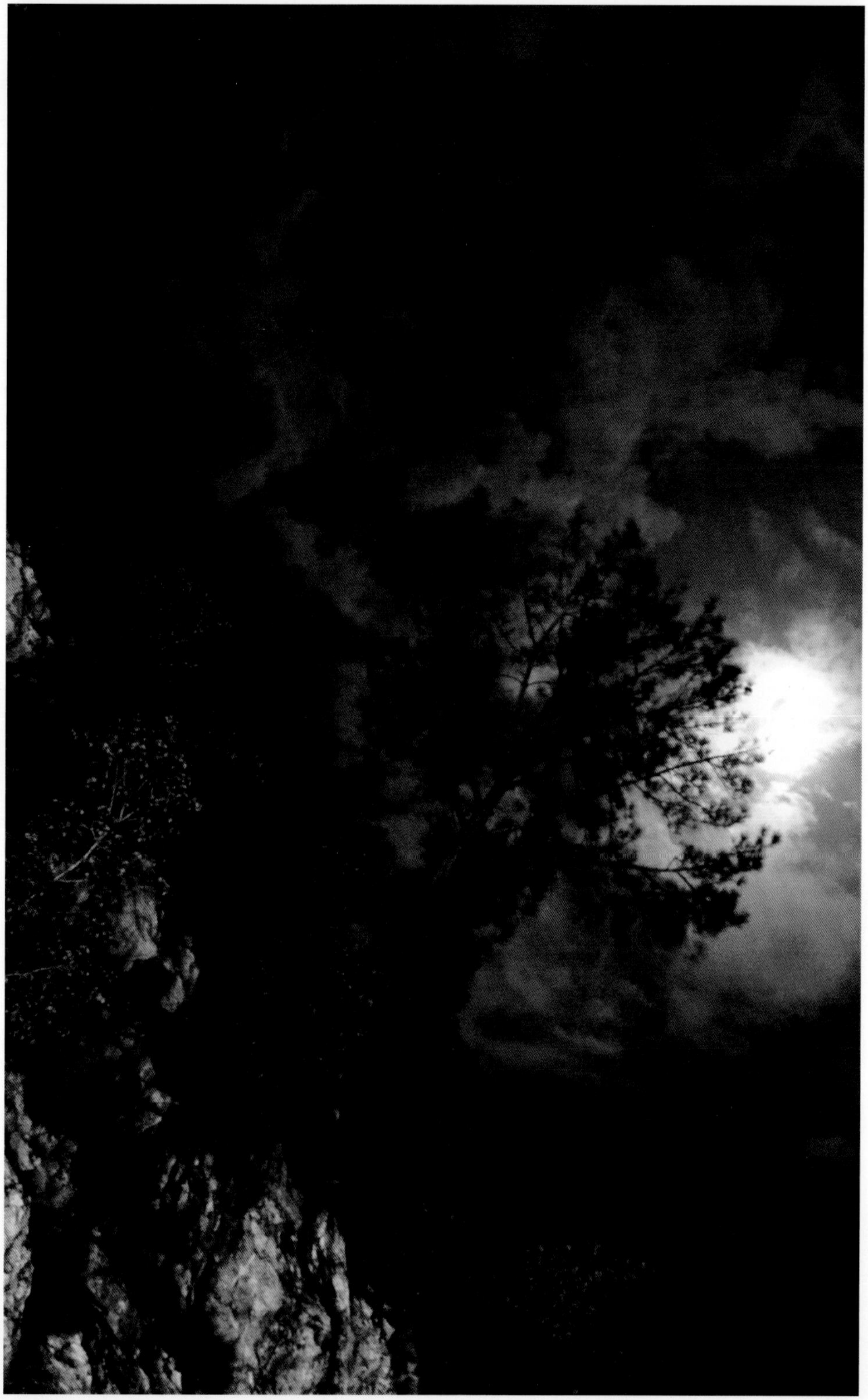

**Well, don't leave me hanging here....what was it?**

>Sorry, just had to stop for a moment because what I saw was so breathtaking........
>
>Oh, it was the mountain! The moon was shining straight onto its face, and every little piece of mica engorged into the stone, every little mica piece was full of light, full of sparkles bouncing between the stone and the stars! The whole mountain face was lit up!

**Oh, of course! Magnificent!**

>I was so stunned that I sank into the grass and was totally transfixed looking at the light show the moon and the mountain were making.

....And there's more....the reflections of all those tiny bits of mica infused in the facets of the mountain's red face focused right down onto and into and throughout me. Every cell in my body lit up with the sparkles of the mica.

It was as if the mountain had entered fully into me, into my experience and was feeling my story.

**Just hold that....too precious for more words.....**

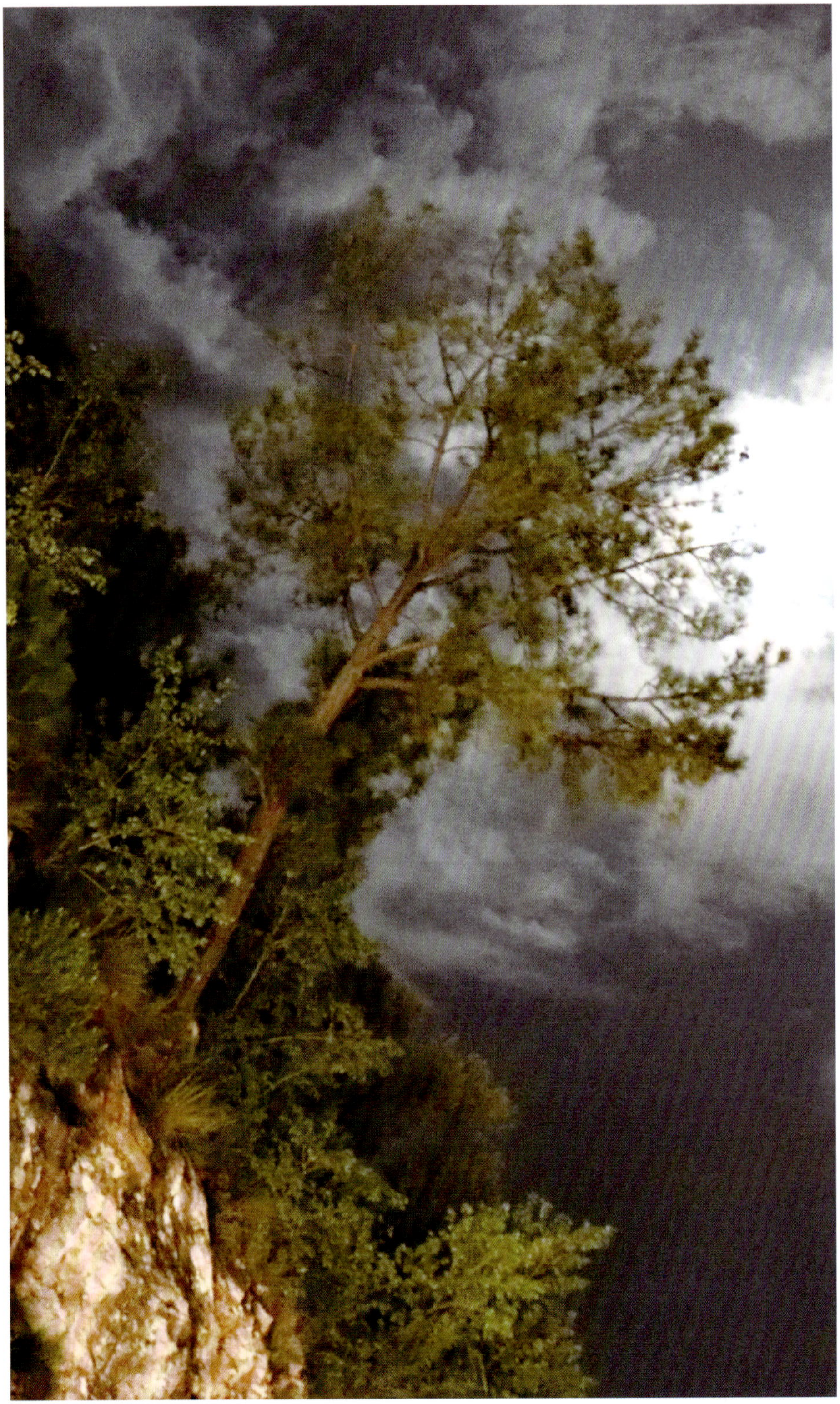

# Wisping

**Are you listening to me?**

        *Whadaya mean? Of course I heard you.*

**You heard the sound of my voice, but did you *get*
what I was saying?**

        *Well, of course! I always do!*

**Do you agree with what I said?**

        *Ummmmm, well, maybe if you say what you
said in another way…..*

**That's what I meant….you heard the sound of
my voice but you weren't listening to what
I said!**

        *…..Oh……………….*

**You know, I feel that often, especially lately.
You're so into telling me how you experience
things that there's not much space for my way to
be expressed…..now, don't get me wrong, I really appreciate how much care and effort you're
taking to help me understand your way. It's just
that I don't feel you're reciprocating, not
stretching my way much.**

        *So, you think that now I've become the tyrant?*

**Well, you said it!**

> *Yes, sarcastically.*

**Reciprocity.....that's what I mean.**

> *OK, so what did I miss that was so important?*

**It is something important, very important. I'm asking for your listening, not your sarcasm.**

> *I'm listening....(sort of!)*

**.....Sigh.....**

**Well, remember that conversation we had when you said something like, "why are there two such different parts in one mind?"**

> *Yes, in fact, I was just thinking about that again just a moment ago.*

**I'll hold the urge to growl back for now!**

..................................................

**That comment you made....I've been thinking about that a lot, and something came to me that seems important. Can you go back to that memory about the mountain....What was happening right before we cranked open the window?**

*"We" cranked open the window?.......hmm-mm.......I'll let that pass for now.......*

*Ok....I'll try to remember. Gee, that was so long ago....but let me see....it was about the same time as the Swiss cheese experience when you did the Neanderthal thing. No, it must have been late spring or so because it was warm outside.*

**Great, keep at it.....**

*I had woken up in the middle of the night and couldn't go back to sleep. This is hazy! I think I was sitting up in bed, oh yeah, I remember. I was sitting there in the dark, and there was a wisp of an idea that darted across my field of awareness, not clear enough to catch its meaning, kind of like a shooting star in a dark sky, but it was strong enough to capture my attention....And then, then next thing I knew I was cranking open the window and unhooking the screen.*

**Oh! This is exciting! Stop here for a moment! What do you think happened to that wisp that had darted past you?**

*Dunno! My mind just jumps to cranking the window.*

**Perfect! Don't you see....it was a Swiss cheese event!**

*Whadaya mean?*

**I remember that part quite well!**

*Yeah? Holy Moly!*

**Oh yeah, well, I noticed that wisp, too! Except it wasn't really a wisp. It was like a light ray piercing into my mind from the mountain, a very strong, sudden compelling urge to go out in the back yard to look at the mountain.**

*You got to be kidding!*

**No, not kidding! It was a flash picture of me—I should say, *us*—standing outside looking at that mountain!**

*So, then "we" cranked open the window and climbed out! Astounding!*

**Yes, well first, the idea came to me kind of like, what do I do about this "wisp?" And then the thought came, "crank open the window and see what the mountain wants!"**

*But then, how is it that both of us remember cranking the window and all the rest. Or, at least I'm guessing that you remember the dewey grass and the glittering mountain, and all that.*

**Well, yes and no. I've been trying to slow things down in my mind. You know how movies work where there are frames that flit through our vision at such a fast pace that it seems like things on the screen are moving in real time?**

*Yeah.*

**I think it's kind of like that. I don't think we merged our consciousness, but we began flitting back and forth between us fast enough that we have much the same memory of that amazing experience.**

*That's wild.*

**Yes, wild indeed! But then there's another aha that I want to share.**

*I'm all ears!*

**Ummmm......well, you know that saying, "what is the sound of one hand clapping?"**

*Yeah, the Buddhist koan?*

**Yeah, think about the question you had a few days back, the one about why any mind would have two such different parts?**

*Oh my....this is blowing my mind!*

**Maybe blowing "our" mind!**

*Kind of I get it....so, you must be suggesting that it takes our perspectives flipping back and forth to create the "movie."*

**Yeah, that it took not only two of us, but as well it took** *two of us with the different perspectives.* **Maybe you're the one that first catches the wisp and draws it down. And then you toss it over to me in your Swiss cheese mode, and when I catch it I weave some of the details into it what to do, like....go to the window and crank it open, and to take out the screen and climb out into the yard....all that. But, don't you see, it takes us both, it takes our different capacities to transform a wisp into an experience.**

*Hmmmmmmmmmm........*

*Have we just made a new movie?*

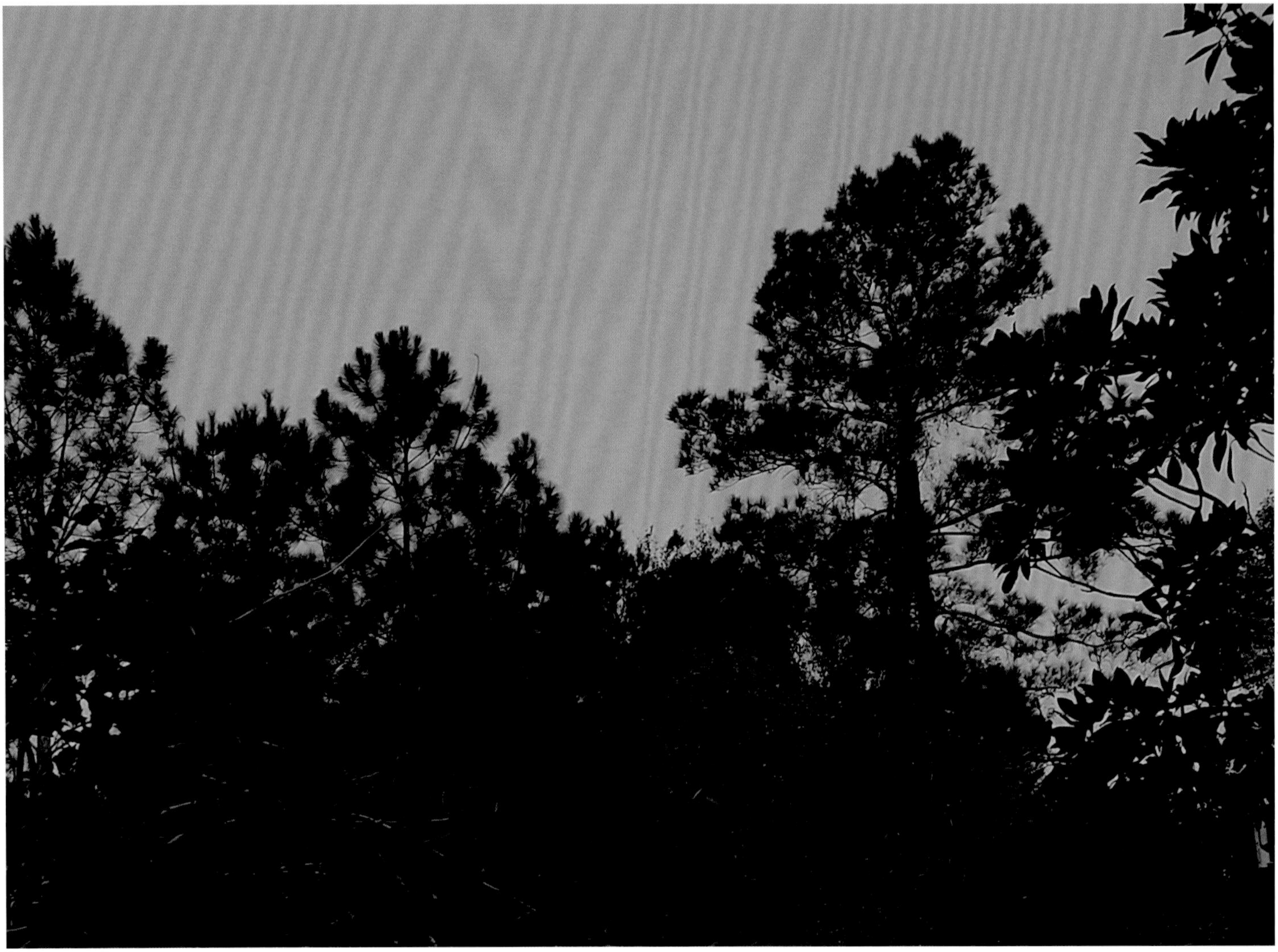

# Close and Personal

**It's so dark I can barely see out here.**

> Ha, ha! Before your usual wake up time! Well, no worries, the light will happen quickly.

**But, what's so important that we have to be up before the crack of dawn?**

> The crack of dawn, that's just the point!

**This better be good!**

*Stop grumbling and pay attention. Now, look over to the right. See that tree on the far side, the one that sticks up the tallest?*

**Yeah.**

*Watch it now, because what I want you to see is going to go like the speed of light!*

**How do I know what I'm supposed to be looking for.**

*Just watch way up at the topmost branches, see....just below the top branch, below the one that's pointing straight up?*

**Ok.**

*OK, just keep your eyes there, because it will just take a few seconds, and then you'll miss it if you're not paying attention.*

**Yes, boss!**

*OK, it's starting, do you see it?*

**No, what?!**

*Look! See, the first rays of sunlight hitting the pine needles at just that spot! Now watch what happens!*

**I'm not sure I'm seeing it.....just a little splotch that looks kind of brown.......oh, yeah, not brown, now it's golden! WOW!**

*That's just the start of the show! Keep watching.*

**Those pine needles in that spot must be at just the right height and just the right angle that they catch those very first rays.**

*Can you feel it....Maybe it's just my imagination, but I can feel those first rays piercing the pine needles with their warmth and their pulsing.*

**Yeah, kind of, yeah, it feels like when I'm in the bright sun and the rays prickle as they pierce my skin.**

*....and now watch how quickly they spread. That feeling is moving through the needles, now to the branches and then throughout the whole tree.*

**It's moving so quickly!**

*I call that tree "The Elder" because it is the first, the sentinel, like a rooster. It's waking up the whole neighborhood.*

**Oh look, it's spreading to the trees next to it!**

*Yeah, and listen the birds are just beginning to sing!*

**Amazing!**

Yes, amazing, and what's even more so is that when I notice that very first penetration of light rays on the pine needles, it gives me a very special feeling.

**Say more.....**

Well, remember when we were talking about the mica sparkles on the mountain?

**That night we climbed out the bedroom window?**

Yeah, well, then I had such a feeling of connection to the mountain and the light coming through the mica sparkles, just as if there was the presence of some kind. Seeing the light penetrate into the pine needles is of that same nature.

The first time I noticed the sun on the needles, it was an "aha!" I feel like I "know" that tree, and it seems to respond to me, just as it does with its branches and needles and other trees. In a way that I can't explain, I'm part of that. It feels very personal.

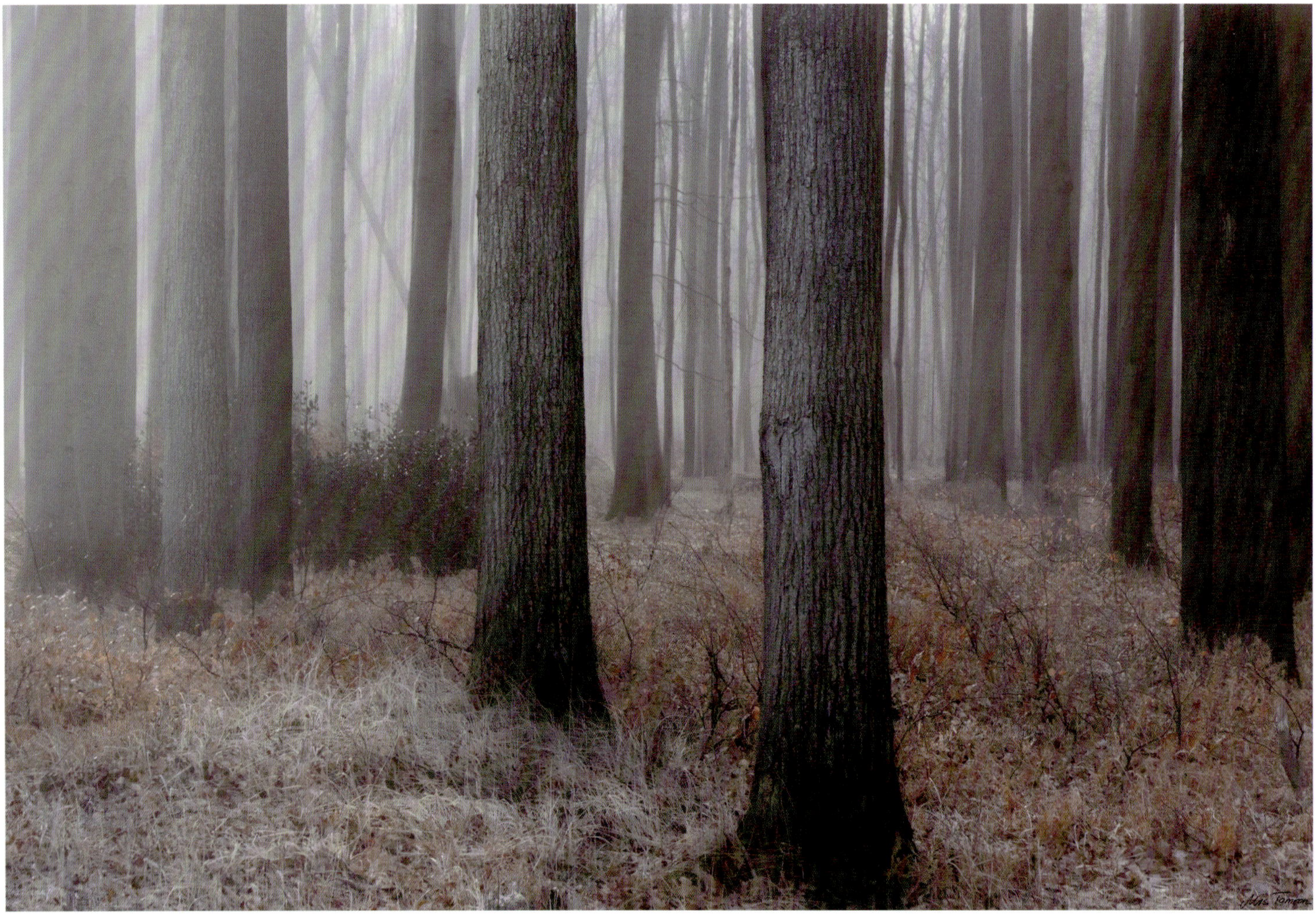

# White Light

**The light here is unusual.....**

> Yes, it's much whiter than the light that usually streams through at this time of day.

**Uh huh...I agree, different than usual.**

> It's so still.

**Yeah, not even a bird sound.....**

> The light is more like a gentle blanket than the yellow light rays that usually penetrate.

**Good way to put it. I do love those yellow zingers piercing me, but yet this is something else, something....oh, what would be the word....maybe *subtle*. But that sounds so intellectual....**

> Ha, ha!

**What's funny?**

> You're funny. Since when do you worry about being too intellectual?!

**Yeah, ok....**

**Well, so, say more about how the light *feels* to you.**

    …..comforting, reassuring, containing, warm, slow, calm. Kind of playful. What about you?

**……immediate, multi-dimensional, very clear but diffused.**

    Could we add "joyful?"

**Yes, pleasant…..satisfying.**

    There's something else….how to put it in words? Do you ever have the feeling that someone is looking at you?

**Um, kind of….hmmm…..you sense that someone is watching us now?**

    Well, not quite. It's a bit like the sense I get sometimes….ummmm….an inkling that you and I are looking from our own vantage points at the same thing. But now it's like an inkling of something being aware of us looking at it, something's connecting with us.

**Wow, the point of a triangle looking back at us?**

What do you suppose this means…is the light looking at us?

**Hmmmmm……**

Perhaps the light just wants to be known, to experience being experienced. What do you think?

**Me? *To experience being experienced….*Well, that's beyond my rational capacity….All I can say is that I think it's just awesome!**

Me, too….I'm awed.

Sky 5

## *The explicate order of things…*

…presents endless opportunities for imposing an array of perceptual and conceptual filters onto the world, giving us a practical grip on things, resulting in consensus reality. Measurement gives us a certain form of security, an "objective" hold on the world—albeit one fraught with severe limitations. Systematic and habitual fragmentation also provides a certain measure of "security," as a means to organize and control behavioral and thought patterns.

It should be noted that what the word "holoflux" points to—both in the quantum domain and the realm of nature—also manifests a certain kind of stability. One could argue that the recurrent patterns and rhythms in these domains are in many respects more reliable than those imposed in our attempts to measure and control the flowing world. In this realm of interwoven movements, the physical world does not—as one might fear—completely dissolve to the participating observer, other than for short moments. Rather, what is revealed is the intricate actuality of constant change, small and large.

Nonetheless, the breakdown of static imagery and thought can be scary and disorienting, especially when one initially experiments with holoflux. Practices grounded in the body such as *rheosoma*, as well as many forms of meditation, can be of great help in adjusting to this flux and flow, enabling one to engage at one's own pace, with one's current capacity.

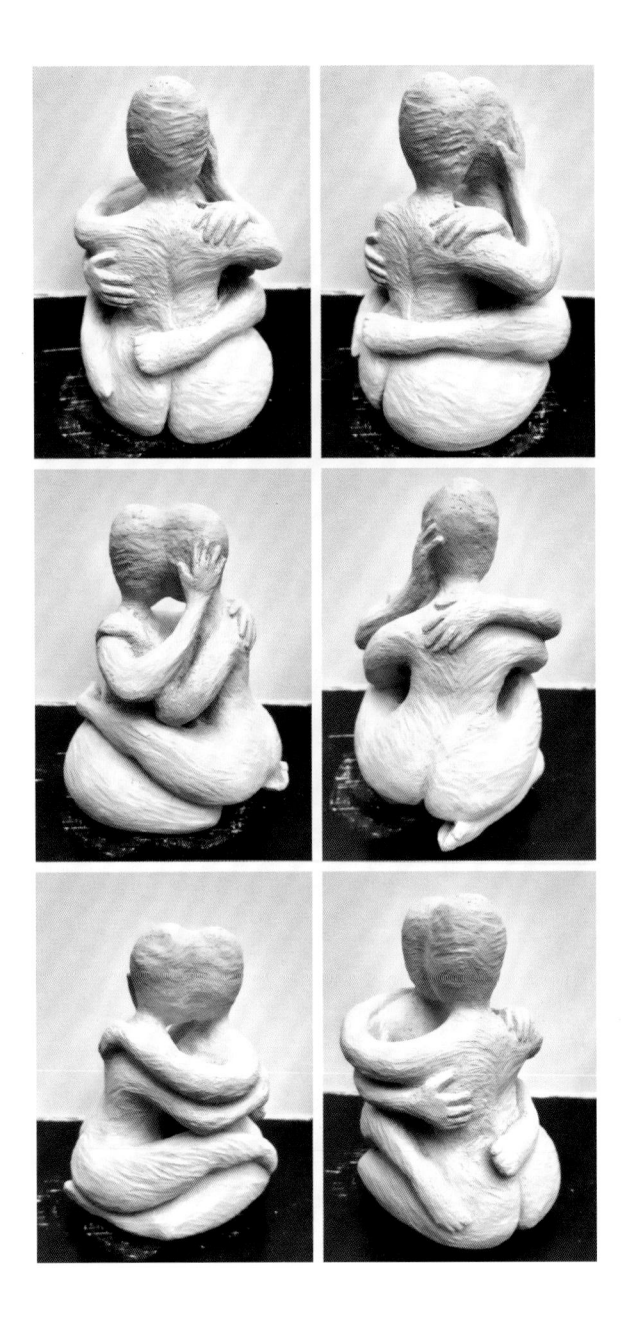

If someone who has not had any early, formative experiences with water is, as an adult, immersed in a large body of water, the immediate reaction will most likely be one of stress and struggle to keep afloat. Rarely is it considered that, under the right circumstance, *imagination* could be key for that person to relax their mind and body, and to find the right posture to start floating naturally.

While each personal experience with holoflux is different, comparable imaginative remedies are applicable to help adapt to this largely unknown territory. It is not, however, as if one randomly imagines anything whatsoever. Rather, one may imagine, and perceive more directly, aspects of what is unfolding from a more subtle realm. This generative imagining is much more porous and open to the flux from which it arises, and allows for varying qualities to emerge over time, giving rise to a more coherent and adaptive re-creation of reality.

This stands in stark contrast to the replicative imagination that we are taught to conform with from early childhood, having us blindly recreate consensus reality that is subtly rooted in measurement and fragmentation.

In light of all this, it seems quite possible to cultivate "flux permanence" as an active complement to the "object permanence" described by developmental psychologist Jean Piaget. For Piaget, object permanence indicates the ability to remain aware of the fact that an object is still present even when we don't immediately perceive it. Here, we are proposing that we can develop the ability to remain aware of the fact that movement is still happening, even when we don't immediately perceive it. As we currently are, subject-object permanence is our collective default. Flux permanence could help to counterbalance this reflexive tendency.

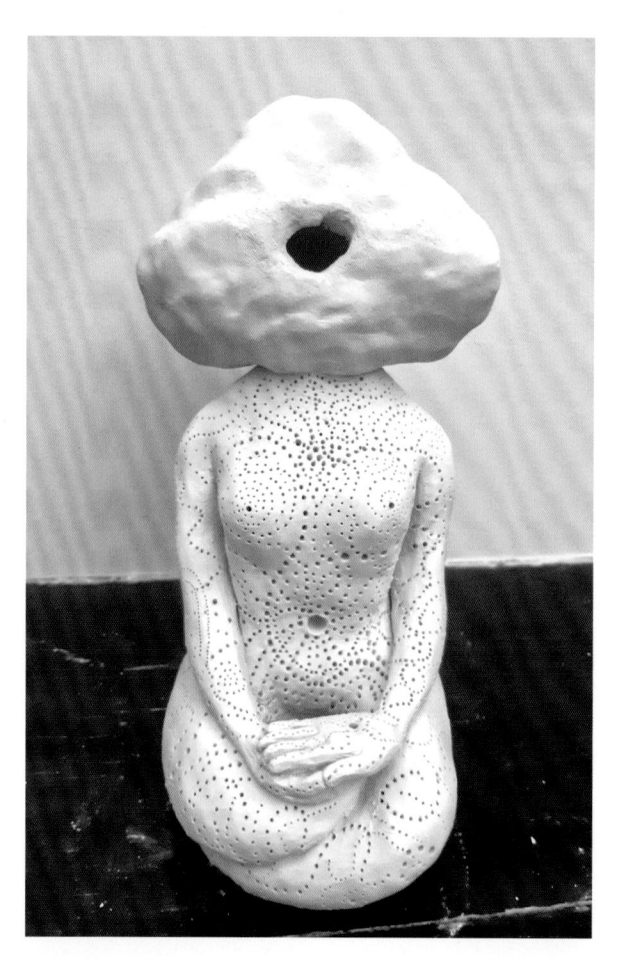

As indicated above, the role of the body should not be underestimated when we work with imagination. Turning attention to the internal processes of the body is one of the quickest ways to get in touch with more subtle movements beneath the veil of thought.

Mind is usually considered the realm of greatest subtlety, while body is considered to be coarse, rudimentary, and ignorant. But denying the innate intelligence of the body is pernicious, and has led us into a pervasive mind-body dualism, both individually and collectively. Ingrained cultural assumptions such as these inform consciousness—and the behavior that ensues.

Mind alone is incapable of fully tuning in to holoflux. If, however, we take mind and body to be poles on a spectrum within this flux, an utterly different perspective emerges. When we become rooted in primal body and mind, enacting primal imagination, our organism can begin to move as an integrated whole—and deeper, more far-reaching meanings can unfold.

When intuiting, sensing, connecting, and not-knowing inspire our basic outlook, intellect and measurement can then serve as useful faculties, no longer dominating our engagement with the living world.

185

# Releasement
(after Heidegger)

---

Richard Burg

# Releasement
# Toward
# Things

# Openness To The Mystery

*a scientist, a scholar and a teacher, walked on a country path, continuing a discussion about the nature of man*

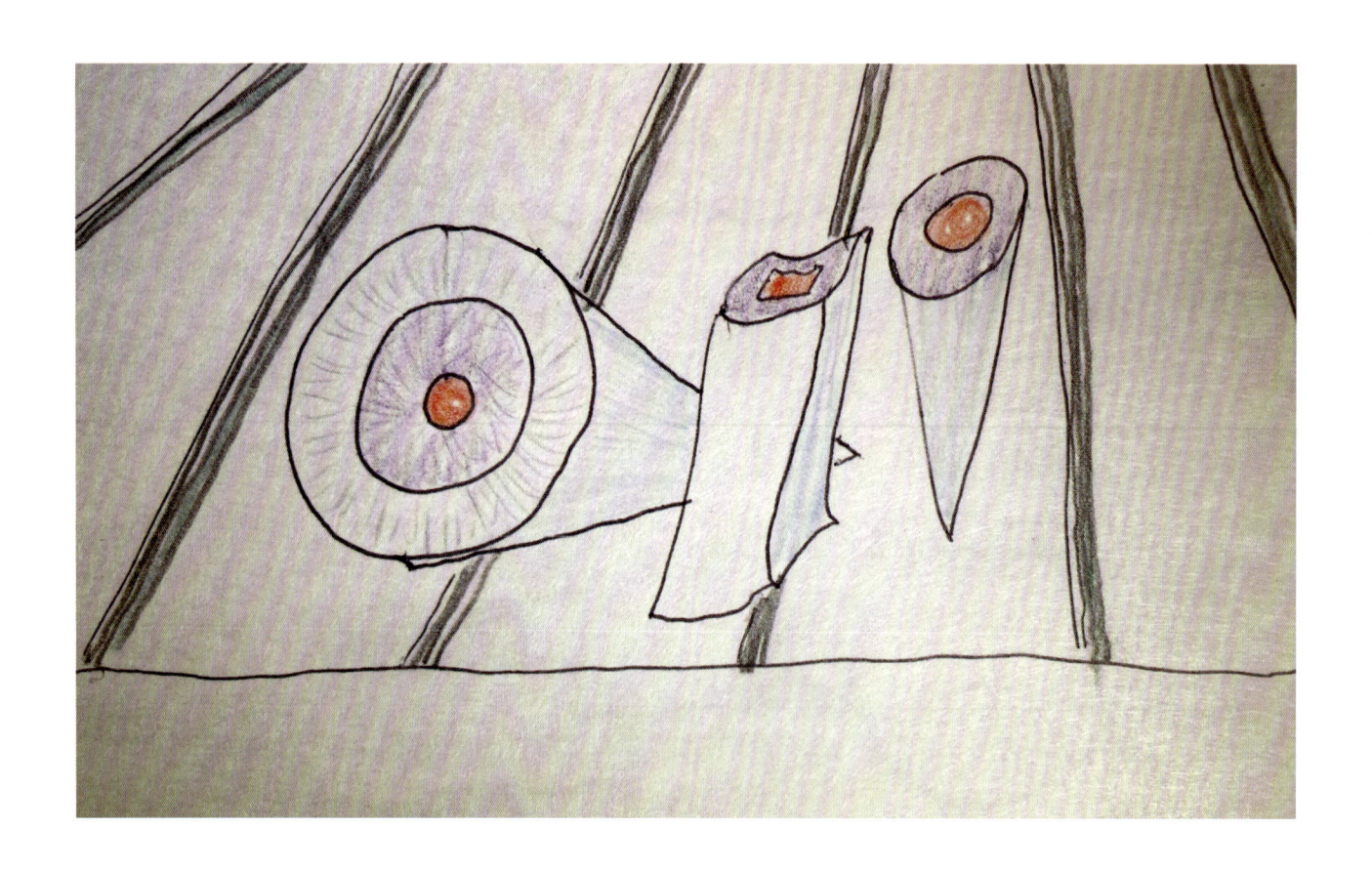

*their walk took them far from human habitation
and into the evening*

*their voices carried across the valley*

the question
concerning
man's nature is
not a question
about man

it is a mystery
how man's nature
is ever to be
found by looking
away from man

can we find man's nature looking
away from man

thinking may distinguish man's nature,
but the nature of thinking itself can only
be discovered looking away from thinking

thinking traditionally,
namely re-presenting,
can be understood as
a kind of willing

to think
is to will,
and to
will is to
think

if the nature of thinking is
essentially something other than
thinking, then it is also something
other than willing

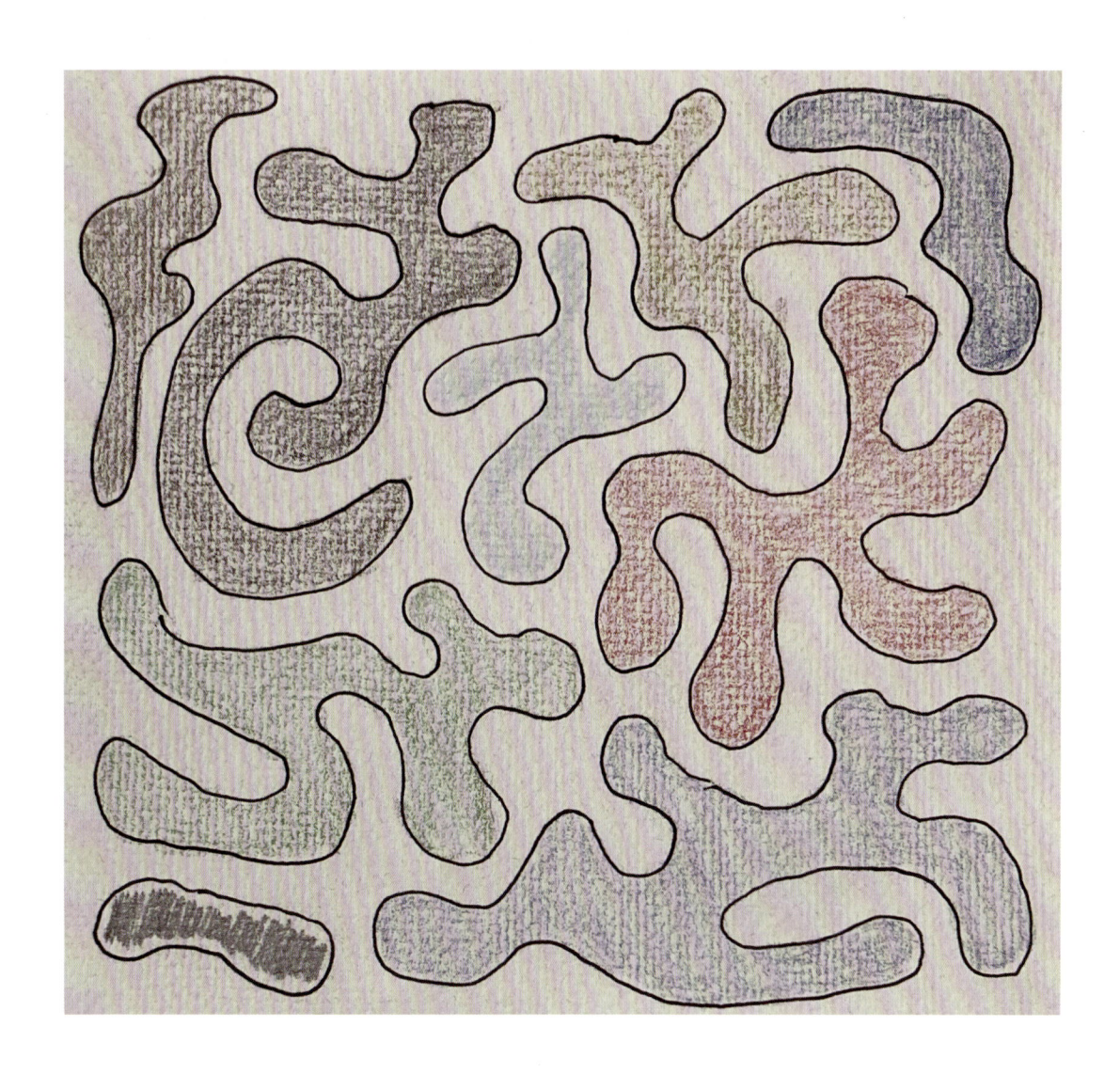

can we discover what we are
seeking through releasement

when we
wean
ourselves
from willing,
we contribute
to the
awakening of
releasement

releasement lies
beyond the
distinction
between activity
and passivity

releasement would be not
only a path but a movement

why does something exist

rather than nothing

our meditation on
thinking demands
non-willing

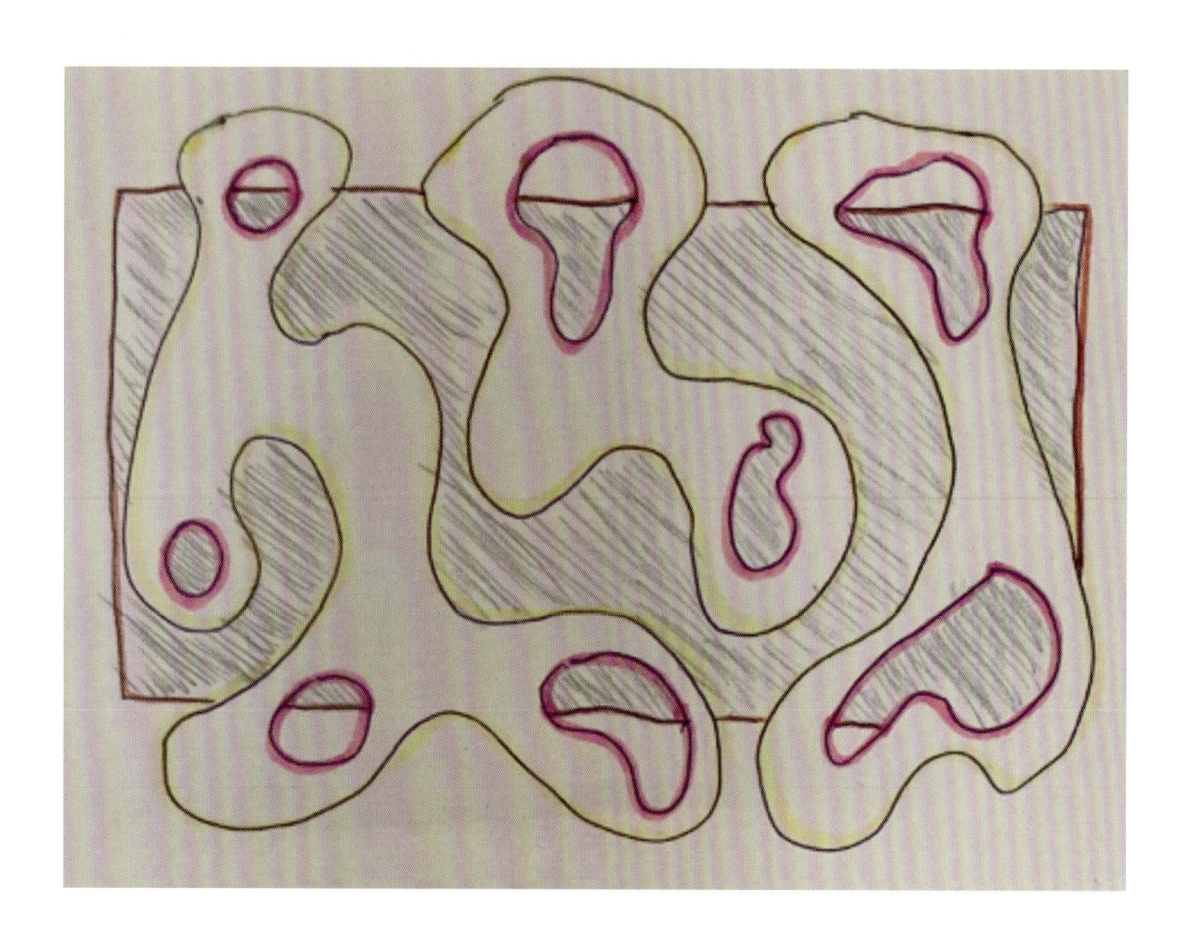

the unfamiliar task

of weaning

ourselves from will

if I embraced
releasement
weaning would
be unnecessary

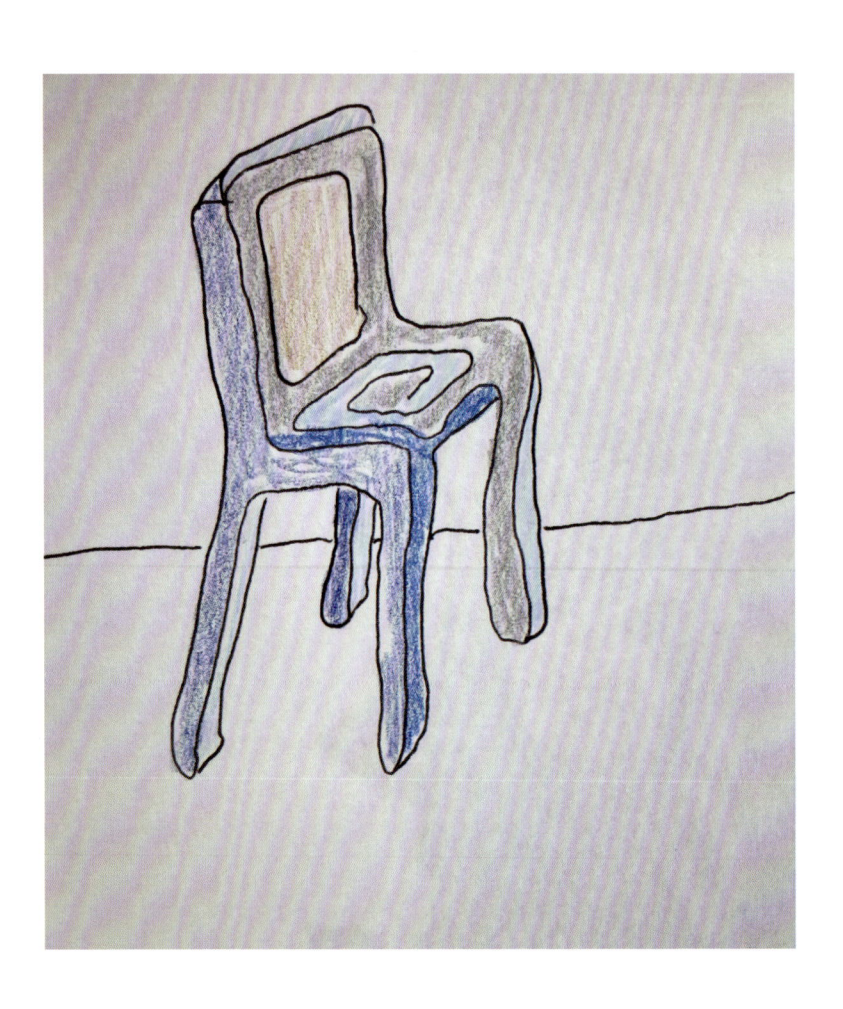

that releasement would lead
to the openness that is all
around us

openness would be that for which
we could do nothing but wait

waiting, but never
awaiting, if we wait we
always wait for something

waiting for vs. waiting without
knowing for what we wait
becomes waiting upon

waiting releases itself into
openness into the expanse
of distance

thinking would be

coming-into-the-near-ness

of distance

the horizon of that which
surrounds us is openness

the openness is not the
result of our looking

the horizon is what faces us out of the openness which surrounds us, full of appearances of what we re-present as objects

openness in which the
horizon of consciousness is
the region

this openness can also appear
as the horizon of our re-
presenting

an enchanted region in which everything belonging there rests there

219

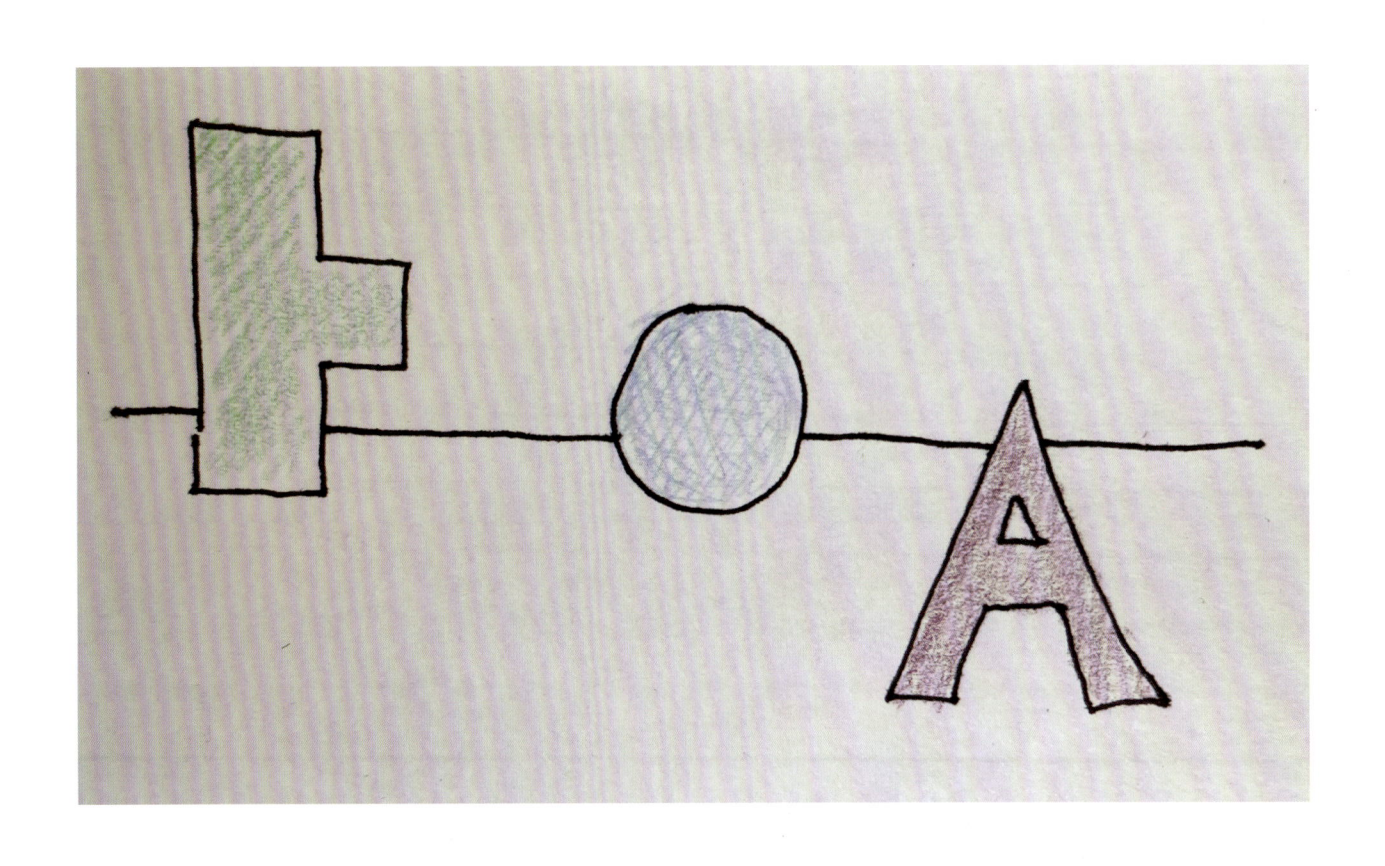

released from and into
that-which-regions

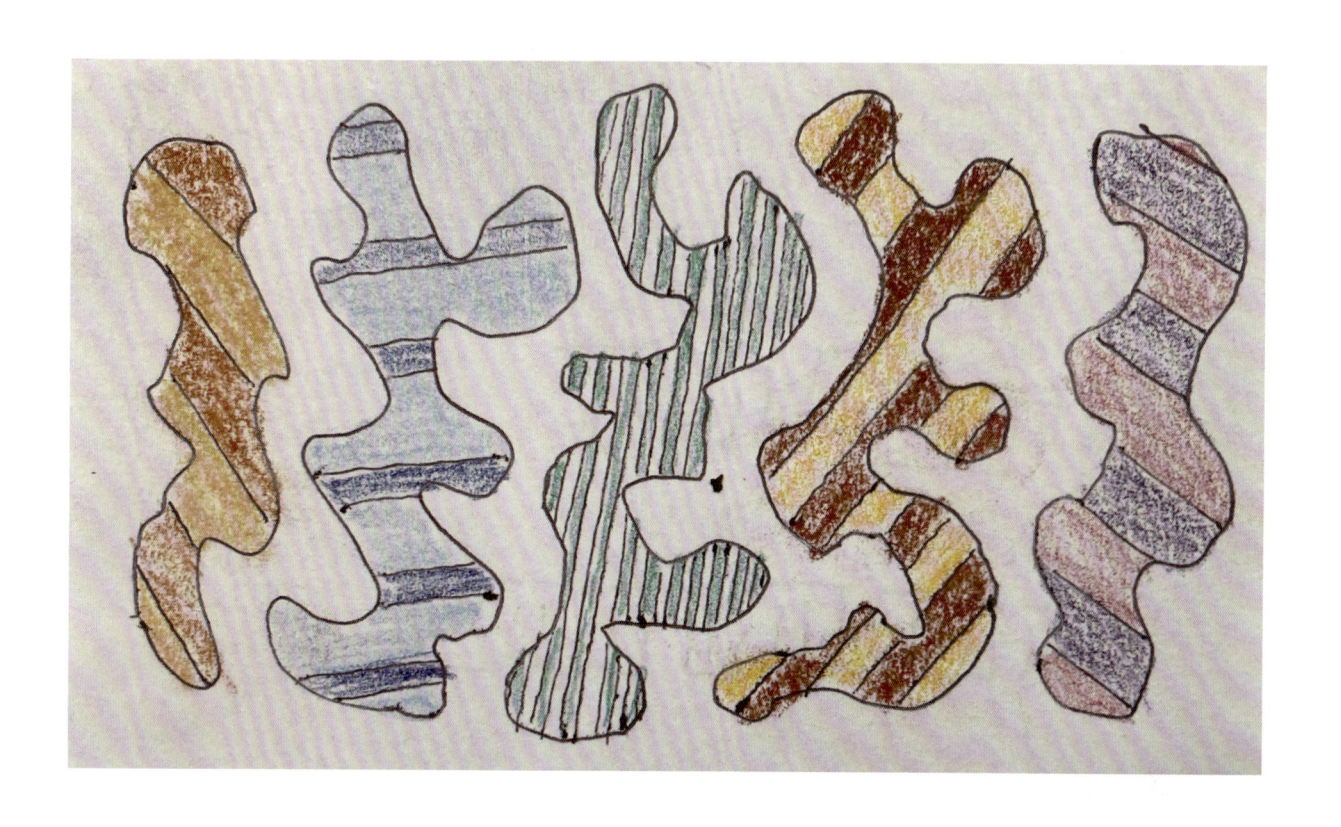

not one among

many but the region

of all regions

the enchantment of this region might
well be the reign of its nature,

its regioning

so we are released into the nature of thinking through waiting for its nature

searching for the nature of the
openness that surrounds us

waiting releases itself into openness

openness itself
would be that
upon which we
could do
nothing but
wait

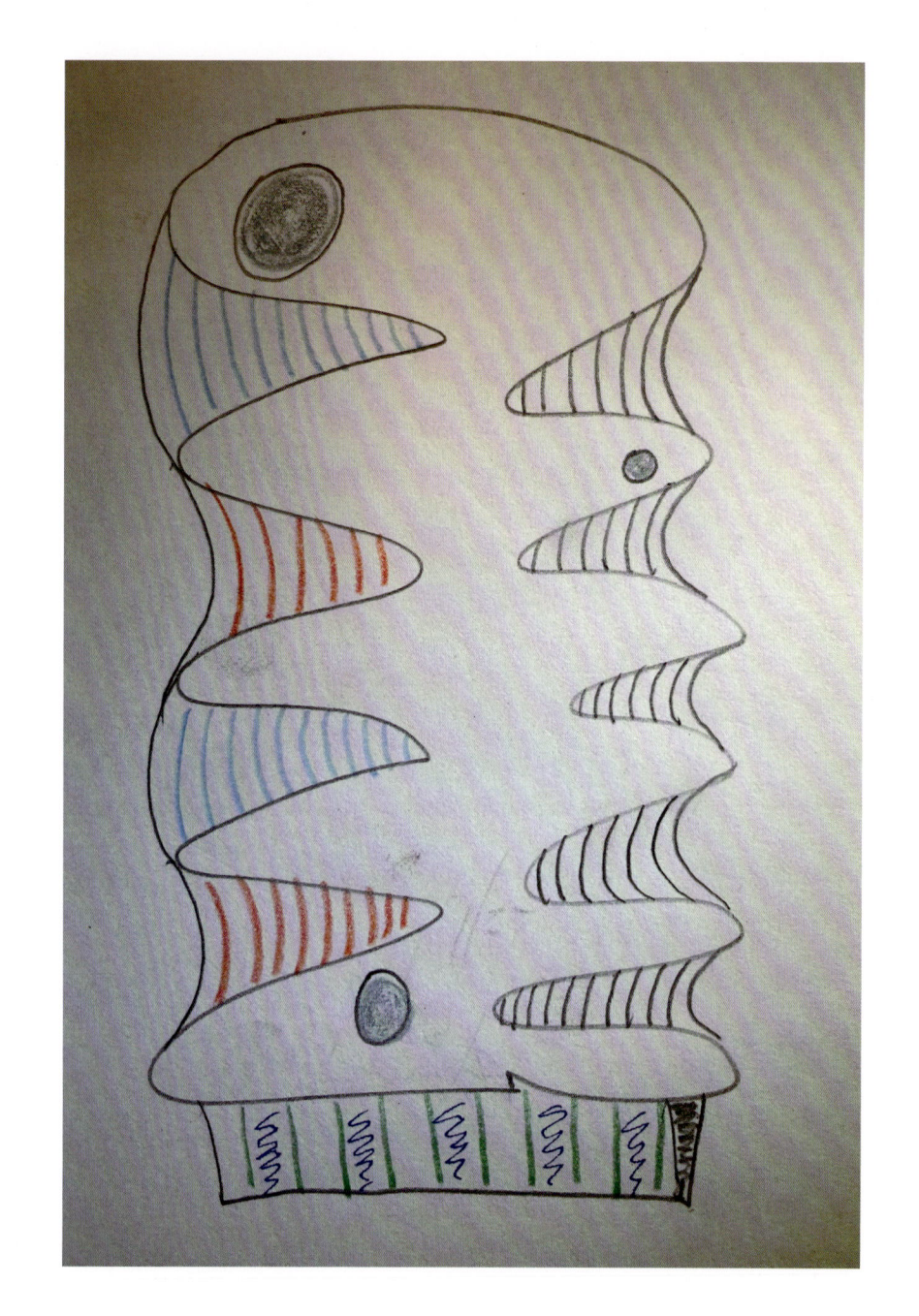

waiting moves into openness
without re-presenting anything

waiting without knowing for what we
wait is to wait upon … a gift

being released into the
nature of thinking through
waiting for its nature

231

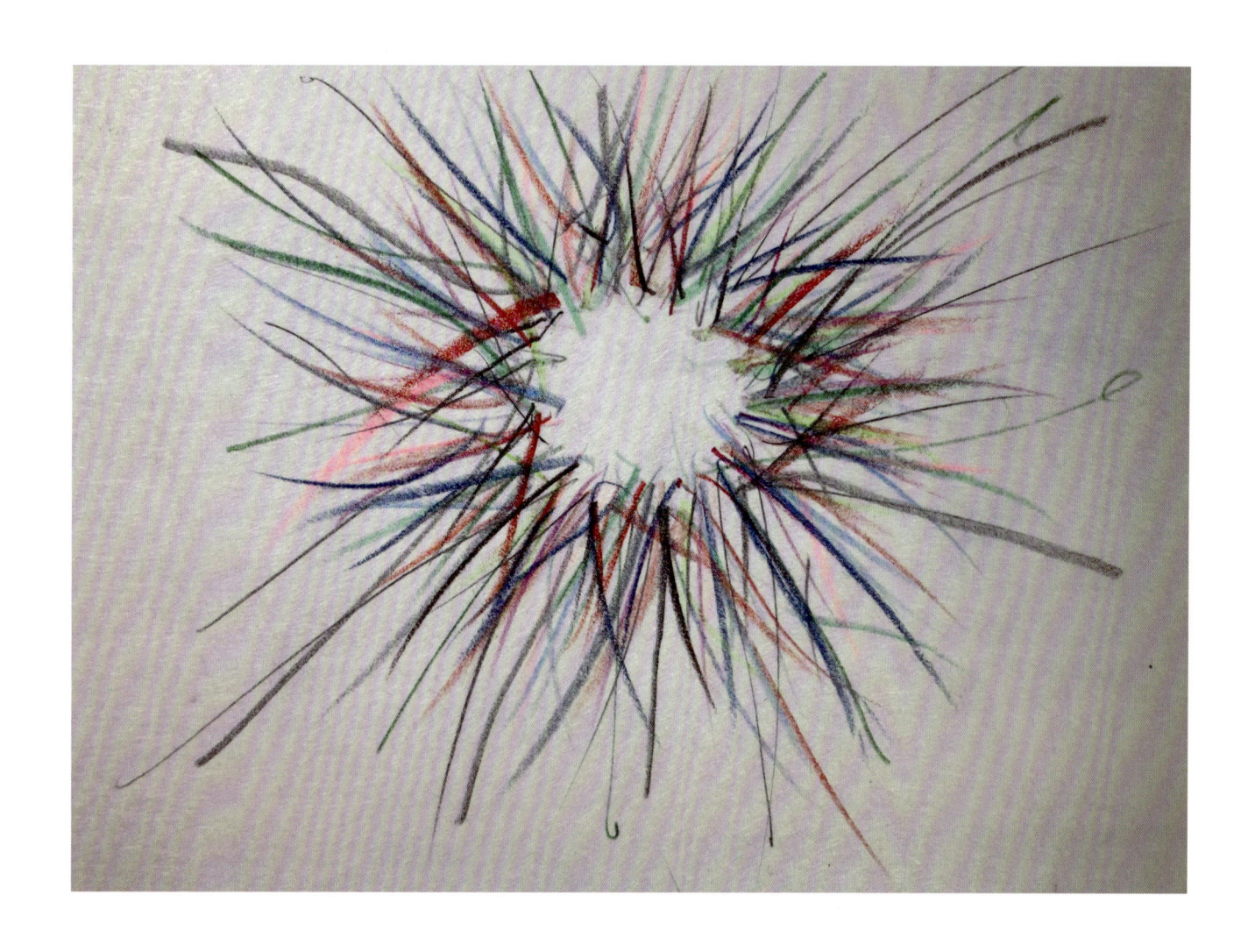

Sky 6

## *To state the obvious…*

Holoflux is present and active everywhere, at all times. It is what we are. How then is it possible that we are mostly unaware of it, that we are not deeply affected by it? The sad truth is that, for most of us in the contemporary world, life is organized in ways to keep us *shielded* from holoflux.

A modern home, or any sheltering construction for that matter, is aimed at transcending the wilderness outside. The subtle wilderness inside us is usually overshadowed by all sorts of distractions: music, television, books, smartphones, computer screens, etc. Even more fundamentally, it is the activity of thought in its broadest sense, as proposed in David Bohm's philosophy, that obscures the innate fluidity of life, of the cosmos.

Of course there are occasional events that can pierce this persistent veil: authentic spontaneity, especially of children and animals; the natural forces disrupting our habits; any kind of animosity in a home; any surge of unburdened spiritual, sexual, or living energy.

Could life not be the other way around, with seminal creativity at its foundation, providing the ongoing context within which daily routines take place?

Art—or any form of human expression for that matter—can allude to aspects of holoflux, as can natural objects or forms that have a certain presence or energy to them. The possibilities are truly endless, and our responsiveness to each variation of form can greatly vary from person to person. Such possibilities can inspire us to engage more frequently, and more deeply, with the unknown that surrounds us, and to inhabit that space instinctively.

Can the prospect of "returning" to holoflux be an open question before us, sparking our generative imagination?

*Overhearing the whole of my surroundings, I cannot help but notice that the sounds of the wind, the birds, the insects, the frogs in the brooks, the quiet cows and horses even, are somehow "timed," generating a spontaneous harmony. It is as if each player involved across the fields is attuned to every other player in nature's orchestra…*

*Surely I am not making this up, am I? The more time I spend with my fellow creatures and the elements, the more my own tune gets in balance and attuned to the whole.*

Walking home, thoughts come and go, like fleeting clouds
I am the frog, I am the wind, I am the sky, I am the geese…
The inner-outer song of holoflux has no set lyric or fixed melody
It simply sings itself, as a flowering, to me, in me, and through me…

# Afterword

*As Bohm and his friend Renée Weber were winding down one of their long and fruitful conversations, they took a backward glance at all they had just discussed, including movement, the implicate order, holoflux, and holomovement. The important thing, Bohm said, was to find a way to "loosen our way of considering consciousness," and that "somewhere we've got to leave thought behind."*

*They indicated that the whole of their discussion was like a pier, "leading us out into the ocean, and allowing us to dive into the depths." It was no use, Bohm said, to linger, to spend endless time thinking about all they had discussed. That, he said, would be like "the fellow who stays on the pier, and never jumps into the ocean."*

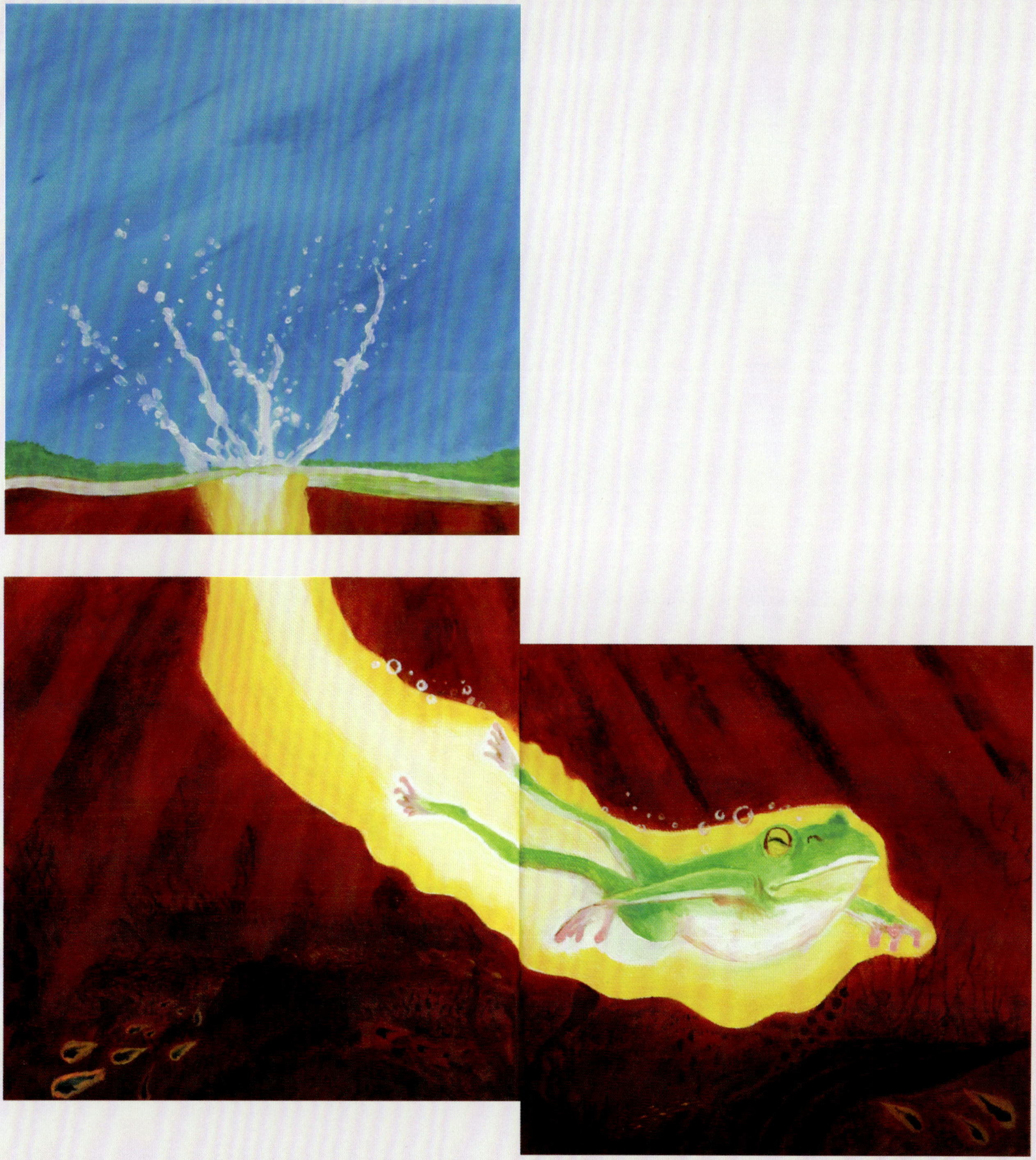

# Coda

There is a storm scribbling
outside    inside
my body
your head
resting in my hand
my left hand cupped
around
the right side
of your perforated skull

# Acknowledgements

Many thanks to everyone who has participated in the Holoflux sessions over the past two years. It was your cumulative energy and intelligence that made this book possible.

Special thanks to all at the Pari Center, especially Eleanor Peat and Maureen Doolan, who were firmly behind this project from the start. And again to Maureen, for her eagle-eye proofing.

Special thanks also to Eva Casey, who has logged untold hours fielding material and laying out the book. Her cover image, *Heliac*, crystallized the contributors' working group as the book began to take shape.

Martin Heidegger quotes throughout "Releasement" from *Discourse on Thinking* by Martin Heidegger. Translated by John M. Anderson and E. Hans Freund. Copyright © 1959 by Verlag Gunther Neske. Copyright © 1966 in the English translation by Harper & Row, Publishers, Inc. Used by permission of HarperCollins Publishers.

There are people way up in the northern plains of North America, right up into the Rocky Mountains. They call themselves Kainai. Nobody knows for sure how long they have been there, but it is a long time. Being of generous spirit, they sometimes speak openly of boundary-crossing, and of flux. Their generosity underlies everything in this book.

# Appendix 1

## Notes on "Intermezzo"
## Beth Macy

*In me there are two souls, alas, and their*
*Division tears my life in two.*
*One loves the world, it clutches her, it binds*
*Itself to her, clinging with furious lust;*
*The other longs to soar beyond the dust*
*Into the realm of high ancestral minds.*

- Johann Wolfgang von Goethe, *Faust Part One*

An invitation to contribute to a book had come to me, something that was to come out of our Holoflux group's explorations into the inner sense of "rheosoma." I was pleased. But much to my distress, no bright ideas came as to what my contribution might be.

On one hand, there were nascent experiences of rheosoma in which I had felt a unique sense of participation with the natural world around me: Sitting in the first lights of morning and feeling the patterns of energy flowing through various types of trees as they indulged in spring's re-blossoming. Or experiencing along with a honeysuckle flower the tickle of bees' feet as the bees forced themselves down the flowers' throats in search of nectar. Or the penetration of sunrays as they prickled mutually the needles of the tallest pine and my own inner body sense. But then, on the other hand, I seemed not able *at will* to bring about the engagement in this new form of participation with nature around me. How did these experiences happen? Certainly, not just at my volition. They seemed to come from some unknown source or process which my rational mind could not pin down.

So, what would I write about in response to this invitation? Finally, in my frustration and distress, our editor Lee Nichol and I talked about my stuckness, and he suggested I enter a "dreamscape." Not knowing what a dreamscape was, I let his suggestion soak.

The morning after that conversation, I awoke early, well before sunlight would begin to stream in between the blinds. That in-between state deepened, and in my floaty awareness I toggled back and forth between dream and liminal fuzz, feeling two different tenors of emotions, a contrariness as if two were arguing. Becoming curious what this was—be it dream or limin—I tuned in to the subtle passionate discord between this unknown pair.

Finally, though still fuzzy, I sat down at my computer, letting the feeling and tonality of the conversation I had eavesdropped upon guide my fingers. Two columns appeared on the screen, and the contrarian feelings formed into words. And then besides the words, images of an intense storm accented the emerging columns of the dialogue, one labeled "Me" and the other "Me, too." And as I began to recognize this divergence of orientation between my two imaginary "me's," the fantasies of their interactions played out in my day-to-day experiences. The vignettes of their growing relationship began to populate my computer screen, and eventually, I shared them with Lee and Eva Casey as a possibility for my book contribution.

Just by chance, soon after having completed my series of vignettes for "Intermezzo," I listened to a Pari Center presentation by Mark Saban, PhD, a Jungian analyst, entitled "Jung's Two Personalities: Psychological Implications" and then read Saban's book, *Two Souls Alas*. Intrigued by Carl Jung's description of his "personality No. 1" and "personality No. 2," Saban had done an exhaustive exploration of Jung's self-described two-sidedness. I was greatly surprised at the similarities my liminal listening had portrayed of my own two-part self and that of Jung's. Saban's presentation guided me into a deeper understanding of this duality that Jung and I, and—according to Jung—*every person*, experiences whether cognizant of them or not.[2]

Jung himself had been aware since his childhood of two parts of himself, parts that were in opposition to each other. These parts were not the results of trauma or early life damage, but as he later came to believe, were necessary partners within a core dynamic that led to his—and any person's—eventual progression toward "individuation" or wholeness of psyche.[1]

Though that core dynamic was a necessary part of Jung's growth and life development, he nevertheless experienced the difference as an inwardly confusing and sometimes difficult dynamic. His personality No. 1 referred to his sense of being an ordinary child and then later an ordinary adult. It was the everyday normal, somewhat mundane, typical person. And sometimes he considered that this part of himself could express, "qualities of meanness, vanity, mendacity, and egotism."[1] Says Saban, as personality No. 1, Jung "existed as merely a grubby, naughty, and lazy little"[1] kid. In later life, personality No. 1 seems to have been quite objective, liking systematic investigation, facts, concrete ideas, and empirical science.[1]

In contrast, personality No. 2 was much more "inward-facing,"[1] self-oriented rather than relational, and was experienced when he was alone.[1] Jung referred to this part of himself as "God's world"[1] in which he experienced nature in its raw, wild form. The "earth sun, moon, weather, night, dreams"...all of those were part of what Jung sensed as "God as a hidden, personal, and at the same time suprapersonal secret."[1] Then, in his adult life, Jung felt personality No. 2 draw him to his deep searching for meaning and his delving into philosophy, mythology, history, archeology, religion.[1] Saban describes this part of Jung's personality: "…it brought with it a sense of timelessness, infinity, and the imperishable, or as Jung puts it, 'superhuman dazzling light, the darkness of the abyss, the cold passivity of infinite space and time, the uncanny grotesqueness of the irrational world of change.'"[1] "He experienced personality No. 2 as a zone of safety and security into which he could retreat, reassured by the comforting knowledge that he alone possessed its 'secret.'"[1]

Jung came to see that our individual life necessity is to form relationship between these two universal parts of self.[1] We cannot thrive when we attempt to inhabit only one of the two sides. Reverberating back and forth between them results in constant conflict and tension or in domination of one part over the other.[1] Rather, the two thrive *together* as they come to form a working relationship. The dominant part eventually must learn to give space and hearing to the subordinate part so that one-sidedness can be corrected and a new way of engaging formed. Of course, conflicts between the two likely continue forever, but the conflicts tend to be worked through so that over time, the third, more balanced position develops.[1] The working through becomes the energy dynamic which produces psychological growth. It is the "motor"[1] of development toward wholeness, or "individuation" in Jung's terms.

Jung and Saban—and perhaps my own two inner parts—suggest that each of us is multi-dimensional. And to borrow from Saban once more, Jung has shown us the dynamic and creative process by which one's ego (Jung's outer, No. 1) and his unconscious (his inner, No. 2) enrich each other and create movement toward deeper wholeness[1] and meaning.

But now, to take this back to my early quandary about what to write as a contribution to a book on holoflux and rheosoma and to my early frustration about "making rheosoma happen." I now see the prescience of Lee's suggestion to try dreamscaping as a way to break through my stuckness. Seemingly, something within me took on Lee's suggestion and displayed within my liminal state a portrayal of the stuckness I was experiencing. Inner parts of myself were at odds, and by giving them space over time within my liminality, they negotiated ways in which to work jointly. In Jung's terms, a third state emerged between them as they squabbled and yet listened to each other, a state of inner participation that I have come to recognize as the basis for my rheosomic experience.

It's when I am able to enter that third state—an intermezzo—and hold the tension between the two divergent parts of myself that, along with the trees, I can feel their regenerating flow of energy at spring's dawn, or prickle with the pine in the morning sun's first penetrating rays, or wriggle with the honeysuckle blossom's pleasure at being tickled by the bees' feet.

## Endnotes / References

[1] Saban, M., 2019, *'Two Souls Alas': Jung's Two Personalities and the Making of Analytical Psychology*, Chiron Publications, Asheville North Carolina, pp. 5-62, passim.

[2] Jung, C. G., 1989, Jaffé, A., ed., *Memories, Dreams, Reflections*, Vintage Books, New York, p. 11-45, passim.

# Appendix 2

---

## A Word After Image:
## Notes on "Releasement"
## Richard Burg

All of the text in the chapter "Releasement" is quoted or derived from the Harper Collins volume *Discourse on Thinking,* by Martin Heidegger. I have lived with this text for over 50 years and found it to be a reliable portal to exploring *thinking*. The text which accompanies the drawings comes from throughout the volume: the translation of Heidegger's *Gellasenheit* by John M. Anderson and E. Hans Freund; the introduction by John M. Anderson; and the Memorial Address Heidegger gave at the 175$^{th}$ birthday celebration of the composer Conradin Kreutzer. Heidegger makes a plea in this address for humanity to embrace *meditative thinking*, not just *calculative thinking*, in investigating the world we live in.

*Releasement toward things, openness to the mystery* is the injunction Heidegger presents in the address. The conversation between three distinct perspectives—a teacher's, a scientist's, and a scholar's—is an exercise in applying that injunction. What is thought?

Over many years, I returned to this text as a reminder of the elusive nature of mind. When invited by Lee Nichol to provide a "catalyst" for our group's exploration of what David Bohm was pointing to when he used the term "holoflux," the Heidegger was a natural element to seed our discussion. I recruited three members of our group to provide the characters' voices, extracted text to create a taste of the experience the Heidegger evokes, and added my "voice over" narrative to connect the dots.

In the present offering, the quotes, transmutations, and restatements are not necessarily in the order in which they occur in the source. In this printed form, the drawings stand for the listeners, the meanings, and the mysteries in the short recital, which provided an introduction for the group's earlier collective examination.

## CREDITS

All collages in "Mountains to Sea" © 2022 Aja Bulla Zamastil

All images in "Letters of Philosophy" and Coda, p. 243 © 2022 Maria Hvidbak

All images in "Bohmian Art School Revolution" © 2022 Hester Reeve

Photos in "Intermezzo" (pp. 137-143, 168-173) © 2022 Beth Macy; photo p. 151 courtesy National Library of Science & History of Medicine

All images and photos in "Releasement" © 2022 Richard Burg, except p.193, courtesy NASA

All images in "Sky" sections and the Afterword © 2022 Sky Hoorne

Introduction © 2022 Lee Nichol

Seed pot impression, p. 92-93, inspired by Acoma pottery

Title page (p. ii-iii)—Western Apache woven basket, circa 1930, artist unknown

**Richard Burg** retired in 2003 from organization consulting, his fourth career (IT, potter, Continuing Medical Education research). His firm, Simple Idea, worked with corporate leaders to integrate human values and productivity in constantly changing environments. In 1990 he joined a Bohmian dialogue group in the San Francisco Bay Area which met weekly during the 1990s. After meeting Lee Nichol, together they designed a nine-hour, multi-day introduction to Bohm's experiment for the first National Conference on Dialogue and Deliberation in Washington DC. In the years following he has been in many dialogue groups—most recently, like many, in online dialogues, before and during the pandemic.

**Sky Hoorne** is a graphic artist and creator of comic strips, and is currently focused on ceramic sculptures, drawings, and paintings. She holds a MS in Computer Science from Vrije Universiteit Brussel and attended LUCA School of Arts Ghent. Sky attempts to make 'inscendental' works of art, in which the viewer is invited to step into the subject by appealing to their generative imagination and subtle participation. This approach involves free play with clichés, perspectives, and polarities.

**Maria Hvidbak** has been a continuing participant in the Holoflux experiments since they began in 2020.

**Beth Macy**—The common thread weaving through Beth's career has been change, having been a manager, leader, consultant, or participant in organizations experiencing difficult issues: organizations from small to large, private to public, non-profit to profit, health care to oil and gas, local to global. David Bohm's dialogue has been core to her research, writing, consulting and teaching for nearly three decades. Beth is completing a book on the ideas and individuals who influenced Bohm's methodology of dialogue.

**Lee Nichol** is a freelance writer and editor. His latest work is *Entering Bohm's Holoflux* (Pari Publishing). He was a long-time friend and collaborator of David Bohm, and is editor of Bohm's *On Dialogue*, *The Essential David Bohm*, and *On Creativity*. He sits on the Advisory Committee of the Pari Center, the Advisory Council of the Indigenous Education Institute, and is a member of the Founding Circle of the Native American Academy.

**Hester Reeve** is a Reader in Fine Art at Sheffield Hallam University UK. Her practice encompasses live art, drawing, sculpture, poetry, philosophy and Dialogue as set out by David Bohm. Hester's work has been shown internationally including at former Randolph Street Gallery Chicago, LIVE Biennale Vancouver, BONE Performance Festival Switzerland, Tate Britain, Yorkshire Sculpture Park, Halle G Vienna and, most recently, Nirox Sculpture Park, South Africa.

**Aja Bulla Zamastil** is an architectural and landscape architectural designer, public artist, and educator. As a Lecturer in the Landscape Architecture and Urbanism graduate program at the University of Southern California, she leads design studios that address adapting our constructed world to shifting natural and socio-cultural forces. As the Creative Director at Watershed Progressive, Aja is responsible for managing and designing landscape projects and educational programs throughout California. These projects explore how we can transform monolithic systems into resilient ecological cycles that re-enchant everyday experience and promote alternative cultural practices.